REFLECTIONS

from Mack Burton

REFLECTIONS
from Mack Burton

Sharing Words of Inspiration, Wisdom and Love

MacArthur Burton

REFLECTIONS FROM MACK BURTON
SHARING WORDS OF INSPIRATION, WISDOM AND LOVE

iUniverse books may be ordered through booksellers or by contacting:

iUniverse
1663 Liberty Drive
Bloomington, IN 47403
www.iuniverse.com
1-800-Authors (1-800-288-4677)

ISBN: 978-1-5320-2631-7 (sc)
ISBN: 978-1-5320-2632-4 (e)

Library of Congress Control Number: 2017910504

Print information available on the last page.

iUniverse rev. date: 07/18/2017

Through poetry, Mack, my husband, conveys his wisdom and innermost self, putting both into stimulating verses that tell stories, express sentiments, and inspire us to live well.

—Gail Elaine Burton

For Elaine, who gives me strength, pushes me to higher heights, and keeps me both grounded and focused. For family, friends, and others who have inspired me and contributed in so many ways. Also for my aunt, Mrs. Willie Mae Agnew, my favorite girl, who has been there for me since … forever.

—Mack Burton

Contents

Author's Note

In life, we all experience events that are forever ingrained in our memories, events so personally profound that they are forever catalogued in either our conscious or unconscious memory. Occasionally, they resurface because of other stimuli: a song, a face that reminds you of something or someone else, or maybe even a dream.

Reflections is a collection of memories of events that were and are uniquely inspiring in many different phases of life and even in death. The influences for these poems come from family, friends, greatly admired ministers, and especially my wife. I have attempted to be very careful in the wording of these poems for one very important, influential reason that I truly believe: you may never know whose life you may be touching, but you should always know that you may be touching lives. It is my wish that something within these poems and the scriptures that introduce each poem will touch you in a positive, inspiring way.

Part 1

A PRIVILEGE TO SERVE GOD

1 Peter 2:9 (ESV)

But you are a chosen race, a royal priesthood, a holy nation, a people for his own possession, that you may proclaim the Excellencies of him who called you out of darkness into his marvelous light.

My Prayer

Father, keep me strong in the word *honor*.
May my heart and deeds always honor my spouse.
May my name always know honor in my dealings with others.
May I always honor those who have been a source of distinction in my life.
May those who honor me by being a part of my life know how special they are.
May You place the seeds of honor in all my endeavors and undertakings.
May You keep my associations and teachings with others honorable throughout.
May I always know that it is far more important
to have honor than to have money,
For money without honor makes for a poor man,
but a poor man with honor is yet rich.
May I always honor my wife's company, and may
she always honor me with her company.
And may my children and grandchildren always
know their place of honor in my family.
May I never become so complacent that I take these honors for granted.
And may You always know the highest honor in
my life is the honor of serving You!

Amen.

1 Samuel 12:24 (ESV)

Only fear the Lord and serve him faithfully with all your heart. For consider what great things he has done for you.

Me and You, Lord

Lord, I know it's me and You
In this new venture we're about to do.

But I pray, Lord, it is mostly You
And You'll help make my dream come true.

For I fear, Lord, if left only to me,
This dream of mine will never be.

For now I've come to understand
The future rest within Your hands.

Amen.

Deuteronomy 13:4 (ESV)

You shall walk after the Lord your God and fear him and keep his commandments and obey his voice, and you shall serve him and hold fast to him.

Not Him

They say we can't talk about Him.
And why should we, anyway?
Just because He is the source of inspiration
That gets us through each day.

They say keep Him out of our schools.
To me, that seems so thoughtless and cruel.
How could you hate and not associate
With the creator of the Golden Rule?

They say we can't talk about Him,
The one who came to save us all.
Yet near the end, we shall see who will cry
For entrance to His kingdom's hall.

They say we can't talk about Him,
Yet He's on all of our money.
Make a fuss over His name, but keep the money just the same.
To me, that seems kind of funny.

But no matter how much it hurts
To see the intolerance of some,
I will pray without cease, for all souls to keep
Every day … until He comes.

For no matter what the prize may be,
Or how they try to present it,
The truth be told, I don't want to win
If God is not in it!

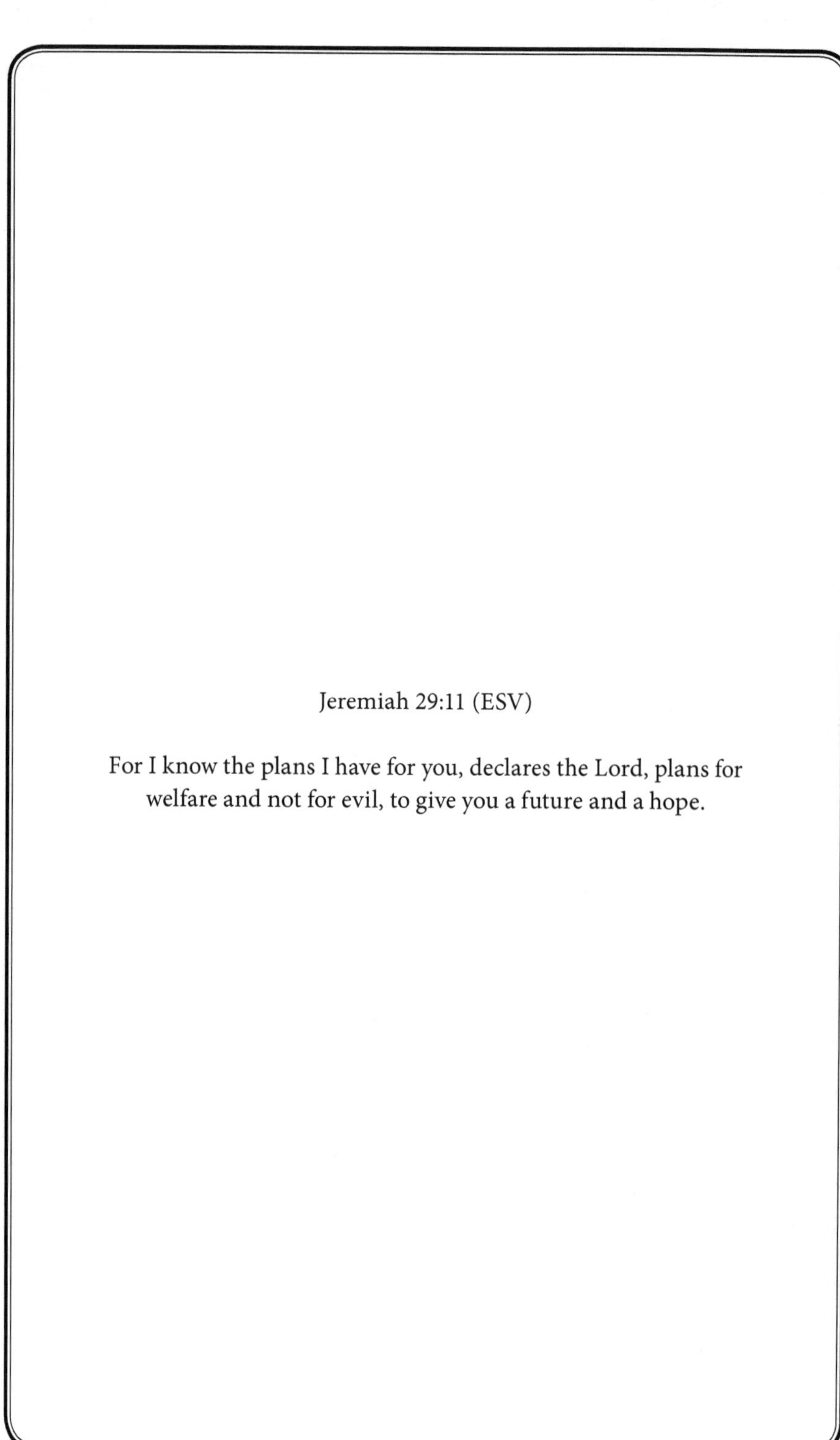

Jeremiah 29:11 (ESV)

For I know the plans I have for you, declares the Lord, plans for welfare and not for evil, to give you a future and a hope.

God Is a Businessman

God is a businessman.
Matthew 25 lays out his business plan.
He tasks us all to take an active hand,
With simple instructions for us to understand.

The lesson was based on the actions of three.
(Our faith is based on the Holy Trinity.)
One wise, one wiser, and one to fear.
Don't miss a great opportunity that's very near.

All power is in the omnipotent three;
Getting to know them is the key.
The course of action that they each discerned
Provides powerful lessons for us all to learn.

A lesson often missed by most
Is that fear to act is a terrible host.
His expectations of us are high;
You can fail, but you must at least try.

This type of fear has never been anyone's friend.
You'll find yourself all alone in the end.
Failing does not make you a failure in His eyes,
For He will bless those who go out and strive.

He put you here not for just something to do.
What He leads you to, He'll take you through
To appreciate the very best in life.
He's going to take you through some toil and strife.

To be sure, He will test your faith;
If He hasn't yet, you just wait.
Yes, God is a businessman,
And we are all in His master plan.

Get ready for some trials in your life.
But His blessings are worth the toil and strife.
Not all of life's joy and mirth
Are meant to be found here on earth.

Some will be waiting when you get to His home,
Like unspeakable joy around His mighty throne.
Yes, God is the ultimate businessman,
And all things rest in His almighty hands.

Part 2

FAMILY AND FRIENDS

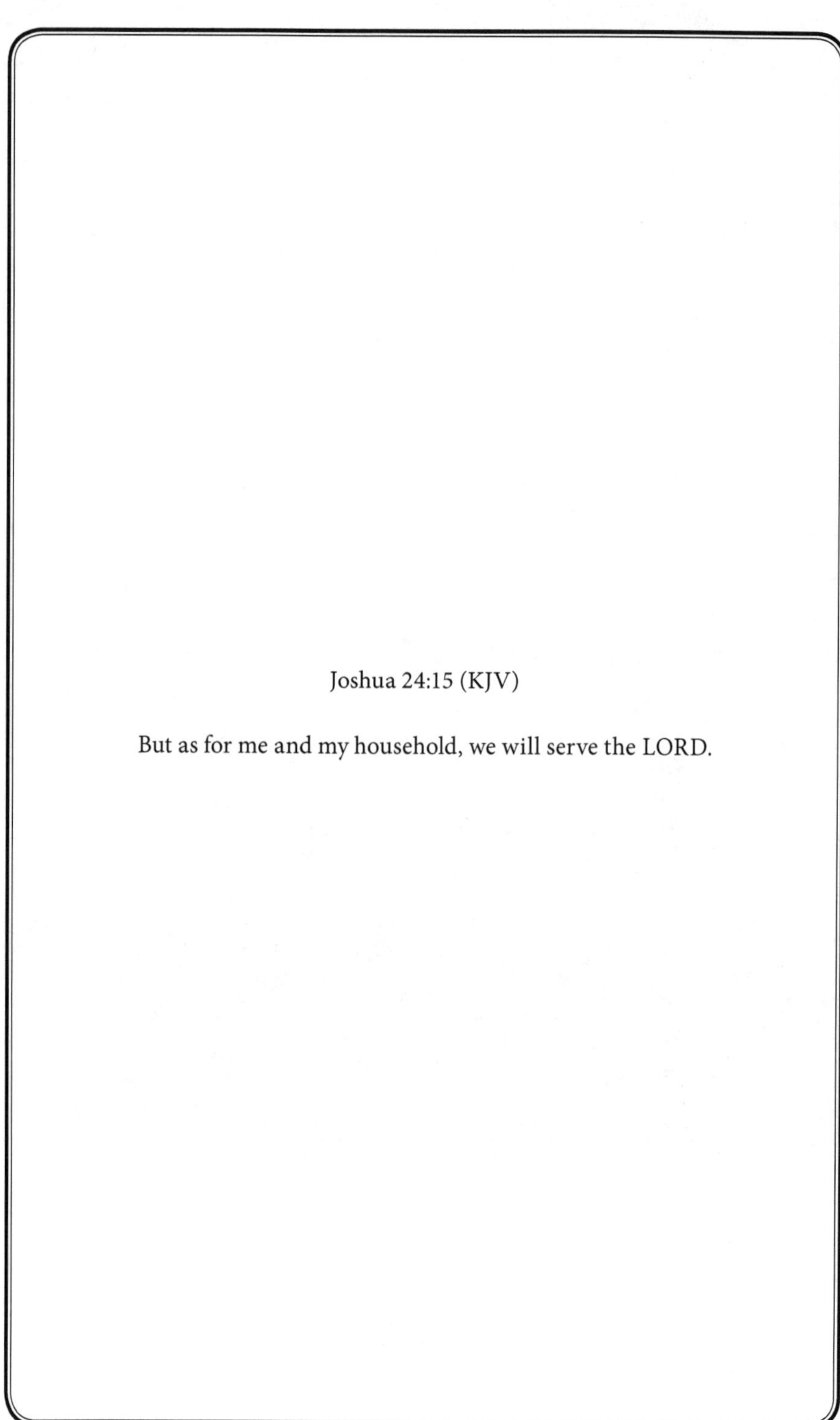

Joshua 24:15 (KJV)

But as for me and my household, we will serve the LORD.

Family

From understanding the ties that bind
To really appreciating a family I can call mine.
From the sounds of laughter of grandkids
To sudden screams of "Now look what you did!"
That's what family means to me.

From outrageous hairdos
To "I ain't thinking about you!"
From Saturday-afternoon cookouts
To Sunday-morning services that make you want to shout.
That's what family means to me.

From the screams and threats to get that homework done
To the long-awaited night when graduation finally comes.
From the painful sadness of a love lost
To keeping the family together at any cost.
That's what family means to me.

From staying in touch no matter how far away
To checking on the elders 'cause you were raised that way.
From chipping in to help for those in time of need
To teaching the young the importance of getting on your knees.
From celebrating the blessings that have come to your life,
Be it brothers, sisters, children, husband, or wife.
That's what family means to me.

Ephesians 6:2–4 (NIV)

Honor your father and mother—which is the first commandment with a promise; so that it may go well with you and that you may enjoy long life on the earth. Fathers, do not exasperate your children; instead, bring them up in the training and instruction of the Lord.

Flowers

I thought about and looked around,
And after a very long search,
The smartest thing we ever did was give our father flowers
While he was still on this earth.

Sometimes we get so caught up
Trying to decide what to do.
There seems to be no end to the changes
Life will take you through.

But flowers are all around us,
And so easy to obtain.
They convey the words and emotions
From which we often refrain.

But flowers don't always have to come
In some type of plant form.
They can be special actions we take
When we deviate from the norm.

Those things we do for those so special
To show how much we care.
Those things we sometimes wait to show
When they're no longer there.

As I look back, I'm so very proud
We decided not to wait
As we presented him love and joy,
His flowers and his cake.

And we can all look back and smile
At his last words, filled with mirth:
"My children are giving me my flowers
While I'm still on this earth."

Exodus 18:7 (ESV)

Then Moses went out to meet his father-in-law, and he bowed down and kissed him; and they asked each other of their welfare and went into the tent.

It's Always Good to See You

I've thought of you so many times
And promised myself I'd call.
But time has always found a way
To slip away from us all.

It's always good to see you,
And always good to be seen,
To remember the times that used to be,
And reflect on what might have been.

I'm happy that your life is good—
Family, friends, and all.
And as for me, I'm doing well,
But I really wished I had called
So many, many months ago
To share my thoughts and all.

It's always good to see you,
And always good to be seen.
My one wish is to see you more,
And with you to be seen.
It's said you don't know what you've got
Until it slips away.
I let you slip away before,
But I will hold on to this day.
It's always good to see you …

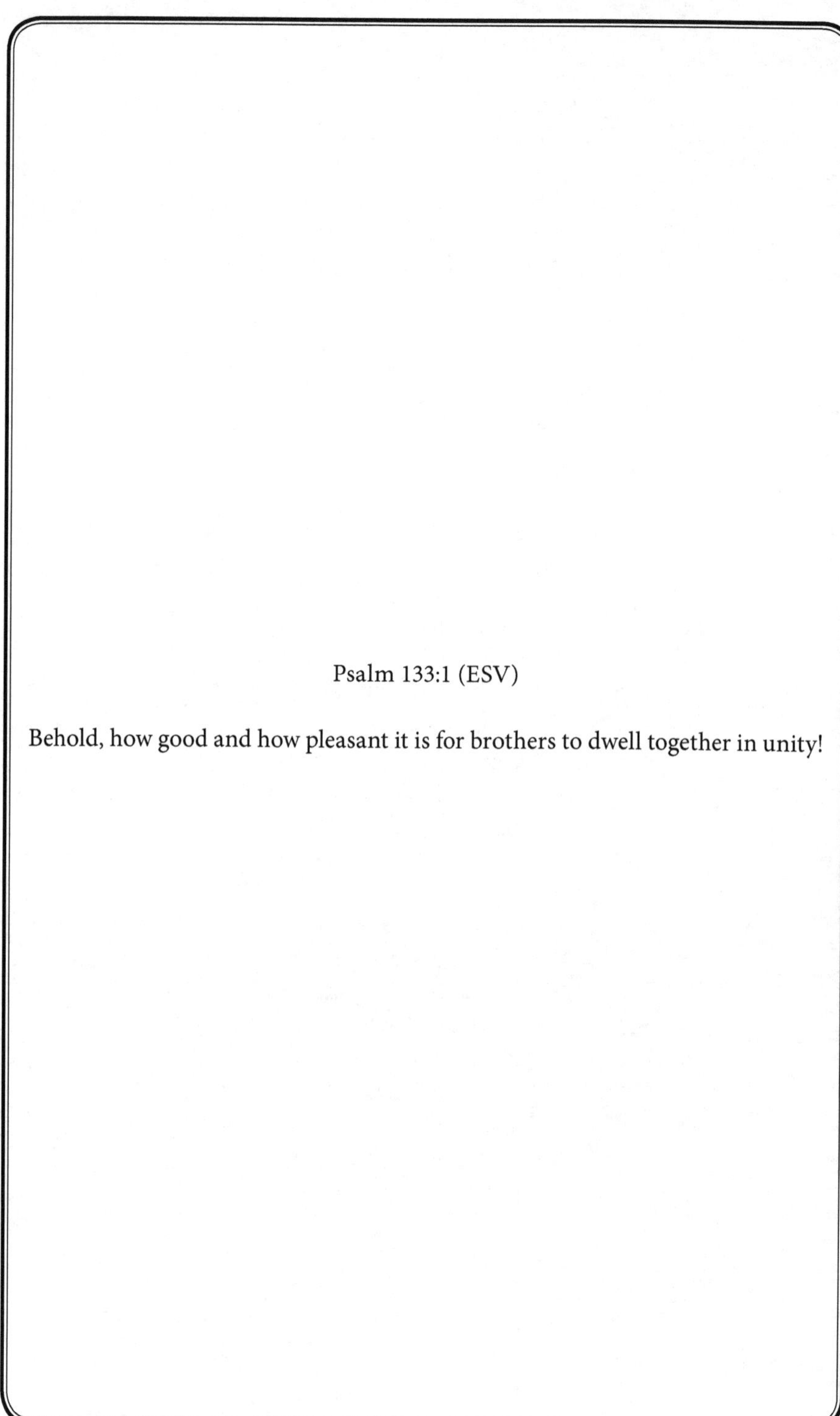

Psalm 133:1 (ESV)

Behold, how good and how pleasant it is for brothers to dwell together in unity!

Jerome

He took me with him always.
"Don't tell," he'd always say
As we'd walk to save the bus fare
And buy treats along the way.

He even took me to the diamond,
Where the big boys went to play ball.
"You can be our bat boy—
Free hot dogs, sodas, and all."

He taught me how to roller skate
Out on our city streets.
He taught me how to dress with style
And keep my wardrobe neat.

He even took me to work with him
When I became of age.
He'd say, "Be nice, and folks will treat you right."
I find that wisdom still sage.

He taught me all about music,
And how to sing and dance,
And how it's important not to be afraid;
Sometimes, just take a chance.

He taught me just so many things,
And I shall miss him so.
But mostly what "big brother" means,
I just thought that you should know.

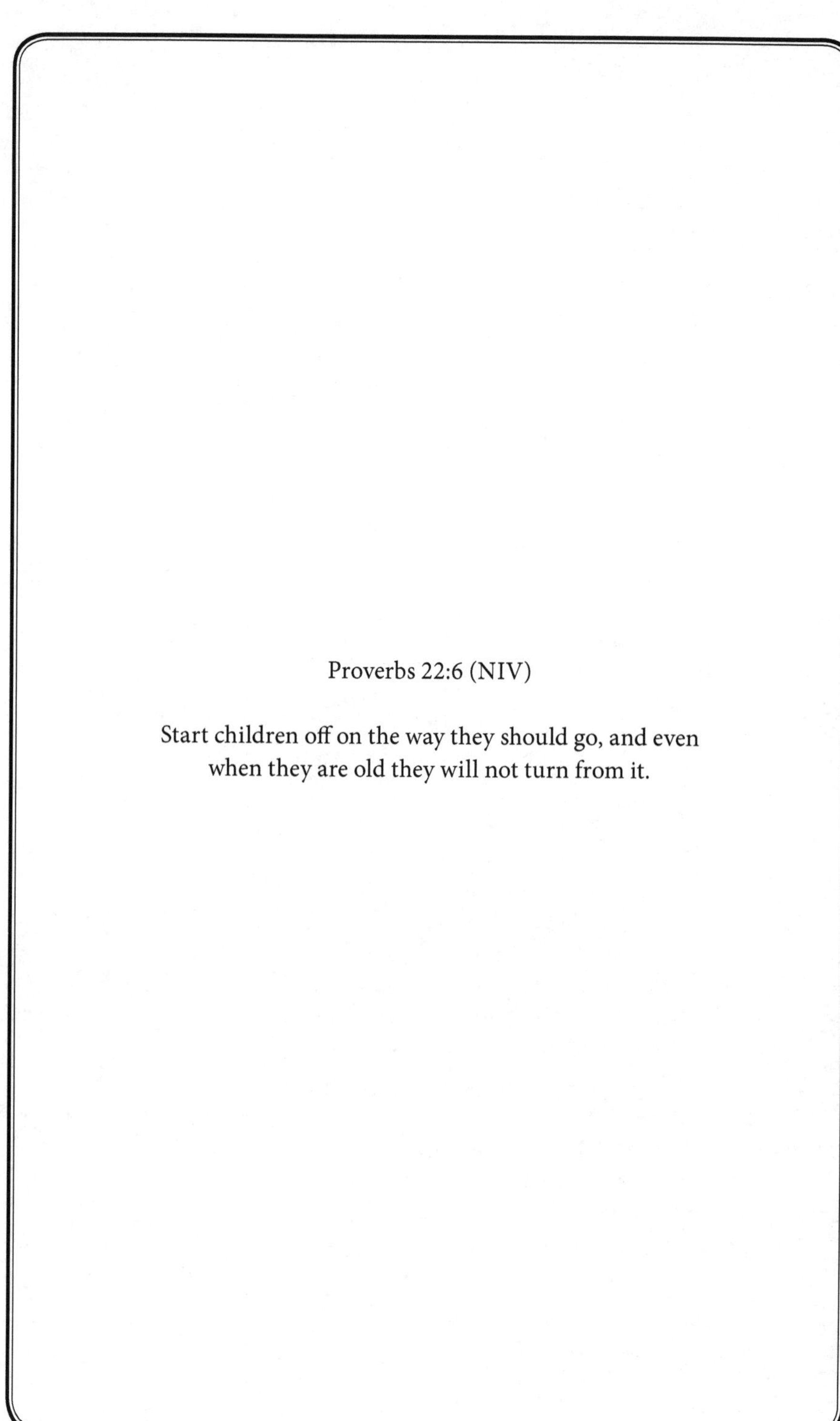

Proverbs 22:6 (NIV)

Start children off on the way they should go, and even when they are old they will not turn from it.

This Girl … My Jen

She's really something special.
I've known right from the start.
She'll make me smile, then drive me wild.
She really worked my heart.

When she was young, to run and play
Was all she wished to do.
From martial arts to the soccer field,
Until the day was through.

And as she grew, her intellect too
Began to soar and soar.
Top grades in school, and playing sports,
Piano, sax, and more.

We'd get on her mother's nerves so bad,
Wrestling and playing around.
She'd always yell, "Stay away from me,"
As we'd tumble to the ground.

But clean a room, put things away,
Or any household chore
Was simply not even in her plans;
It all seemed such a bore.

Computers, music, cell phone, and of course her TV.
MySpace, iPod, Sidekick—a techno junkie.
College is an evil; work is even worse.
Just let her have her music, hear her quote each verse.

We laugh, we play, we fight; sometimes there's nothing to say.
And though she may not realize, I love her anyway.
I'm not her biological, but I couldn't be more proud.
God has blessed me even more by making her my child.

Proverb 13:20 (NIV)

Walk with the wise and become wise, for a companion of fools suffers harm.

Circle of Champions

My closest friends are champions;
I surround myself with such.
They build me up and encourage me
With support that I need so much.

Champions share their special gifts.
They're not selfish with their blessings;
They're more than happy to share with you
The benefits of their life's lessons.

Champions relish the thought of assisting,
Whether coaching, lecturing, mentoring, or just listening.
They're not afraid to tell you to avoid wretches,
And you reach your best through perseverance and stretching.

They catch you before you can fall,
Help you back in the circle, spotlight and all.
And I do the same in return,
For I'm not so smart that I still can't learn.

I know I have gifts to share too.
There are many things that I like to do.
What a blessing to have champions as friends,
Here in a circle that knows no end.

Genesis 8:22 (NIV)

As long as the earth endures, seedtime and harvest, cold and heat, summer and winter, day and night will never cease.

Summer

Summer sings her song again,
And I look forward to fun times with friends
June bugs fly, and the robins sing,
And young lovers prepare for a summer fling.

Lazy days move oh so slow,
Bring contemplations of where to go:
To the park or to the beach;
Maybe to the mall, just to purchase some treats.

To the city to visit with friends,
Or to the country to see family again.
No thoughts of school and little thought of work.
Just loving life and laughing till it hurts.

Long, lazy naps when the sun is high,
Enjoying evening meals under the night sky,
Music floating on air throughout the day,
And sounds of joy from kids at play.

Thanking God for the gifts He sends.
A twinge of sadness as summer nears her end.
The only fights are with water balloons.
The only sadness: summer's gone too soon.

Part 3

NUGGETS OF WISDOM AND KNOWLEDGE

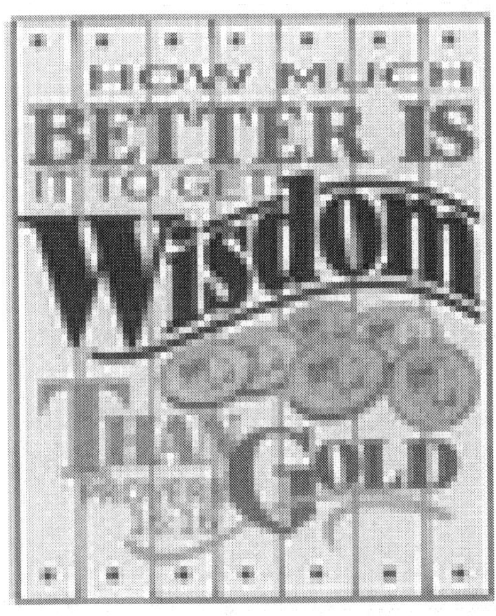

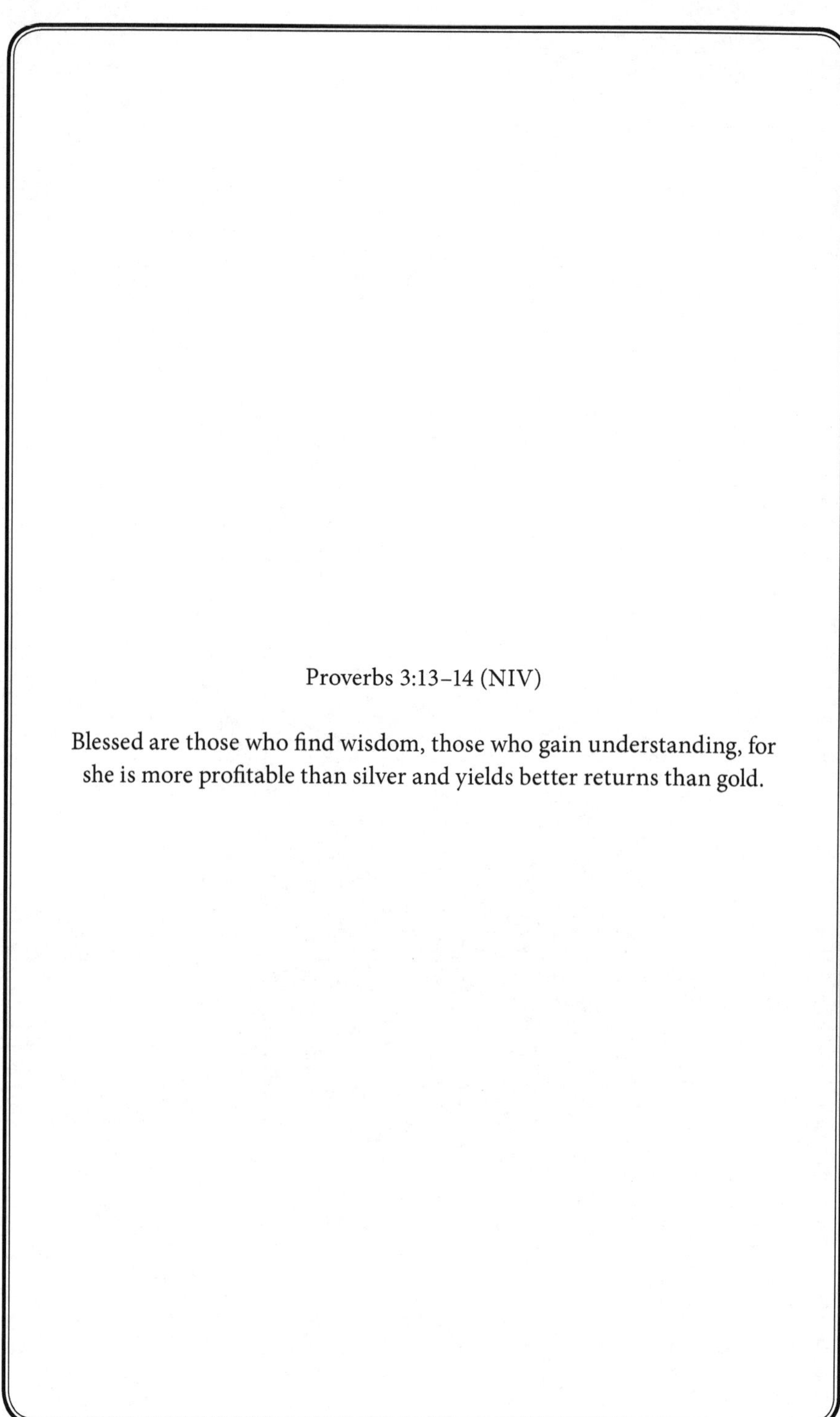

Proverbs 3:13–14 (NIV)

Blessed are those who find wisdom, those who gain understanding, for she is more profitable than silver and yields better returns than gold.

I Blame No One but Me

(Originally published in *Twilight Musings*)

I blame no one but me
For the successes or failures in my life,
For I realize that joy rides with pain,
And success is often followed by strife.

I blame no one but me
For any goal that I don't achieve;
If I lack preparation, determination, or motivation;
Rewards I don't deserve to receive.

I blame no one but me;
I point the finger at no one else.
If I decide to take my dreams
And place them on a shelf.

I blame no one but me
If my relationships don't grow strong.
If I take no initiative to bring us closer,
I deserve to be alone.

I blame no one but me
For how I live this life,
For God gave it to me alone.
I dare not lose this fight!

Proverbs 15:1(NIV)

A gentle answer turns away wrath, but a harsh word stirs up anger.

Excuse Me

What did I say?
What did you hear?
Could be two different things.
We hear through filters
And process meanings
Based on what we feel.
Emotions sometimes clouds our hearing,
Completely changing the meaning,
Where what you hear and what I said
Are different for different reasons.
What did I say? What did you hear?
Depends on your state of mind.
If I speak nice, and you hear right,
We'll get along just fine.

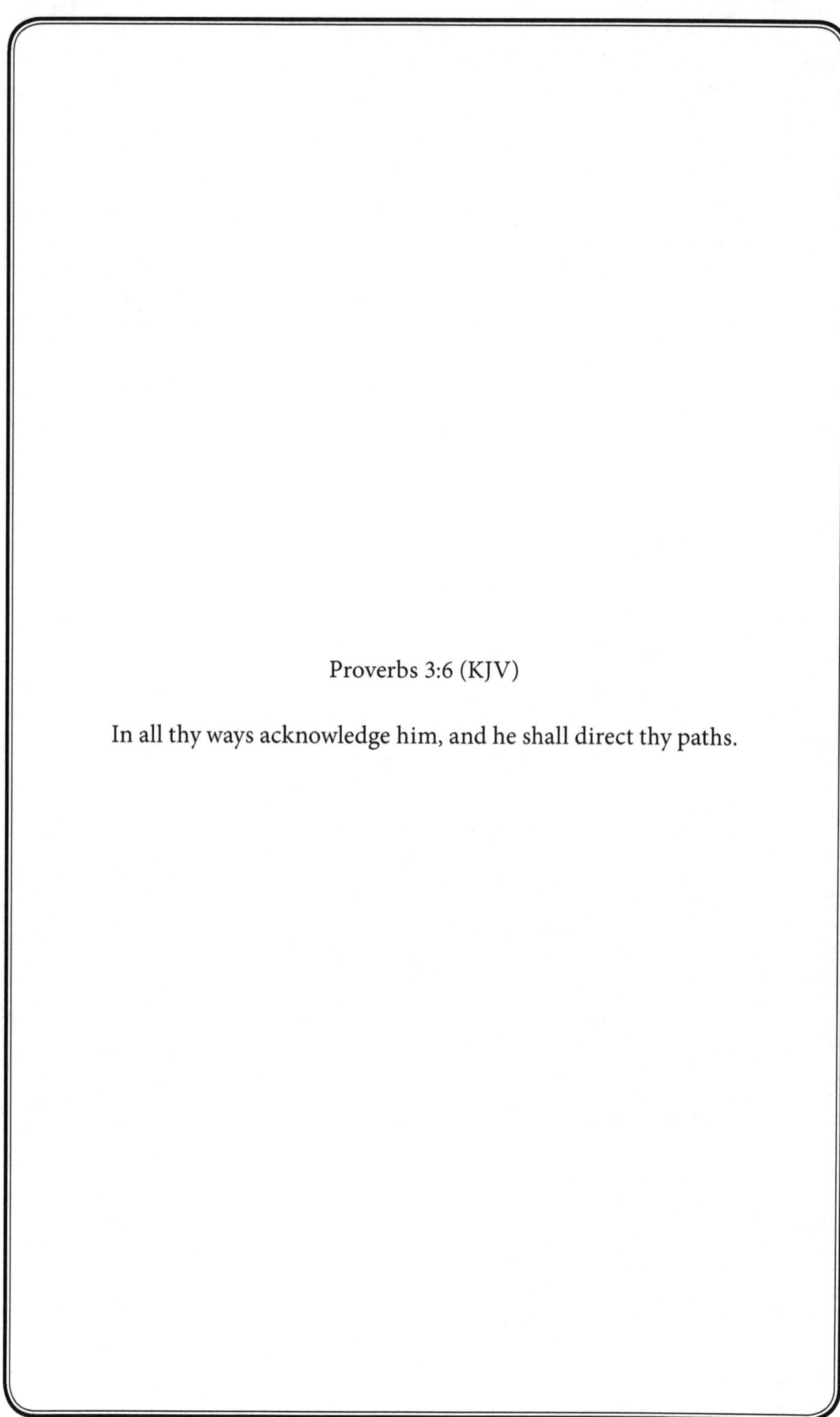

Proverbs 3:6 (KJV)

In all thy ways acknowledge him, and he shall direct thy paths.

Searching

Sometimes it just sits right there,
For all the world to see.
It's totally up to you
To be or not to be.

Sometimes it's buried very deep,
Way down below the surface.
Work hard to raise it, or let it go.
You decide: Is it worth it?

Others may see it clearly;
You may not see it at all.
Yet sometimes when we least expect it,
God reveals it all.

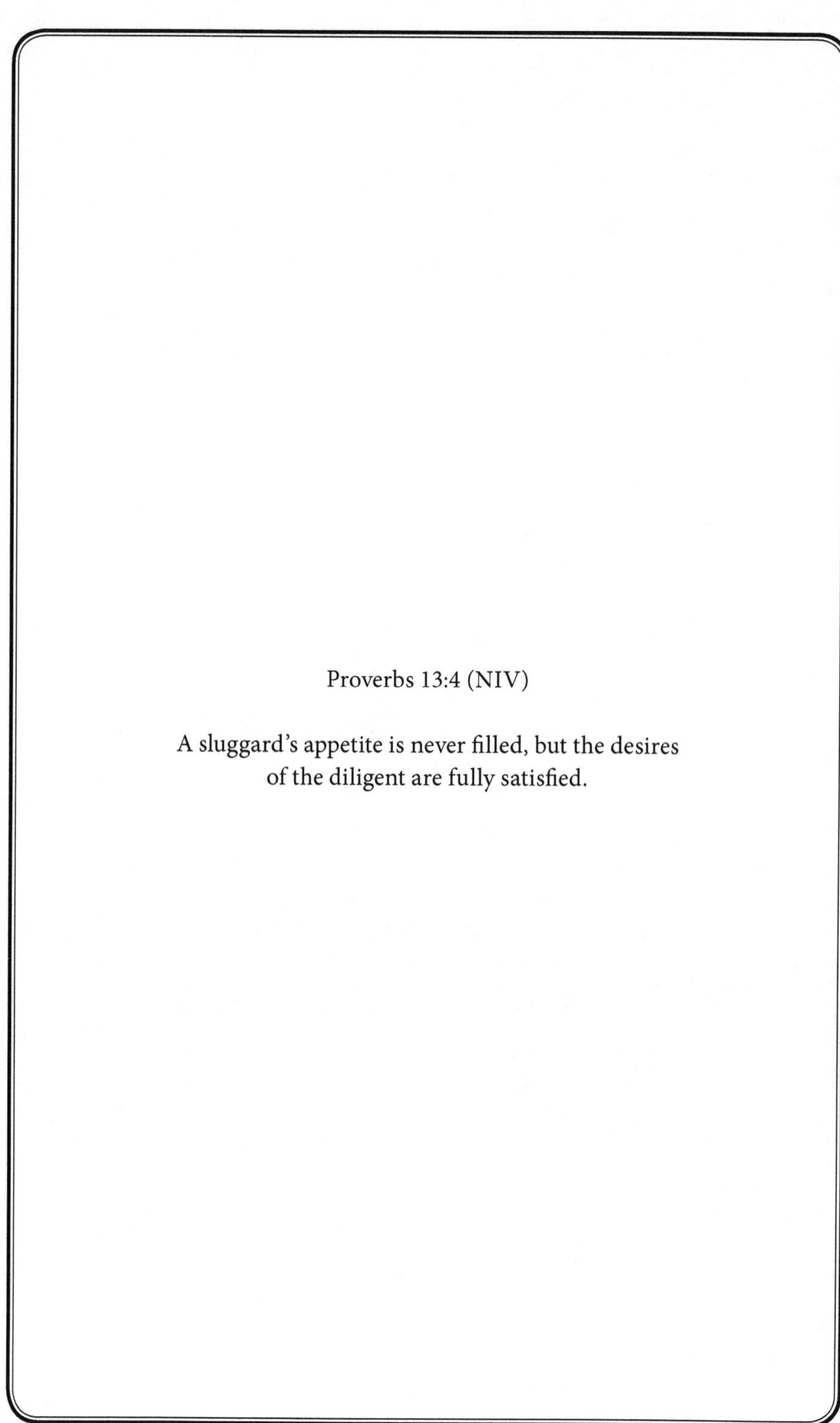

Proverbs 13:4 (NIV)

A sluggard's appetite is never filled, but the desires of the diligent are fully satisfied.

Easy

I went in search of easy,
From the comfort of my couch.
Just waiting for fortune to come along
And give my name a shout.

I knew I had a due season,
Thought sure my time had come.
But easy must have taken the bus;
It seems to have been long gone.

Life is not a revolving door
That opens and closes with ease.
Life is a series of locked doors,
And each one requires a key.

So off the couch and on your feet,
There is much work to do.
Easy left town on a fast bus.
It was not looking for you.

Galatians 6:9 (ESV)

And let us not grow weary of doing good, for in due season we will reap, if we do not give up.

Good

What does good look like?
Maybe you didn't hear me; let me turn up the mic.
I said, what does good look like?
Is it working out a problem without starting a fight?
Or maybe giving in and confessing that someone else is right?

I ask you, what does good look like?
Is it rushing to a quick answer and turning it in?
Or taking time to work the problem to ensure you can win?
Is it working alone in secret, and claiming credit for yourself?
Or involving your team and then spreading the wealth?

Somebody, what does good look like?
The ever so slight turn of a lover's head,
Or the tender sweet sound of a spoken word?

Tell me, what does good look like?
The well-groomed and articulate CEO,
Or some special mentor that you've come to know?
A beautiful child all excited at a piano recital,
Or a glorious sunset that you delight in, in idle?

Please, what does good look like?
Could it be a warm touch when your heart is broken?
Or a financial boom, not just some mere token?
Someone special who accepts you, faults and all,
Who lifts your spirits so you can walk tall?

Tell me, what does good look like?
If good is the goal, and better tops that,
But best is supreme, so that's where it's at.

Then tell me, what does good look like?
Is it the people and things that last through time,
And with age get better, like some fine wine?
When you search and search, but what you find
Was right there in front of you all the time—
Yes, what does good look like?

2 Corinthians 5:17 (ESV)

Therefore if anyone is in Christ, he is a new creature; the old things passed away; behold, new things have come.

New Life

Tell pity and despair to move out of the way,
And let divine inspiration rule and have its say.

Know that new life starts today.

Life comes at you fast, and opportunities don't last.
To the swift go the spoils, so let the dye be cast.

I say new life starts today.

Live life for today because tomorrow is not promised,
And to thine own self you must be totally honest.

Let those special in your life know how special they are.
Keep them close to you; don't let them drift too far.

Friends and lovers are few and are gifts from God.
Let them know they have a special place right in your heart.

New life starts today!

Proverbs 16:16 (ESV)

How much better to get wisdom than gold! To get understanding is to be chosen rather than silver.

Choices

For every choice, there is a consequence;
That is a proven fact of life.
The decisions you make can bring you joy,
Or create heartache and strife.

Choices that are made in haste
Are often not the best.
It's really better to take your time
And just let the decision rest.

Consider the consequences
From every possible position.
Understanding based on your choices,
You'll have to live with the conditions.

Also with the knowledge that
Your choices affect more than just you.
Family, friends, and loved ones
Are often involved too.

Choices made in haste
Are often such a waste.
For once you realize your mistake,
More actions you must take.

Redo a job, repair a heart,
Or mend a broken friendship.
Choices and their consequences—
Be careful, try not to slip.

Philippians 2:3–4 (ESV)

Do nothing from rivalry or conceit, but in humility count others more significant than yourselves. Let each of you look not only to his own interests, but also to the interests of others.

Negativity

You tell me all the shouldn'ts, the wouldn'ts, and the don'ts/
You say, "I don't think that will work; if left to me, it won't!"

You never have an encouraging word, from the beginning till the end/
Yet you tell everyone you see, "Yeah, girl, that's my best friend."

I need someone to support me in all my goals and dreams,
Not someone to convince me that I have unworkable schemes.

Why can't you just get on board and share this ride with me?
You may be surprised; it may open your eyes to how bright your future can be.

And all it takes is faith and work.
Lose the negativity.

Ephesians 2:10 (ESV)

For we are his workmanship, created in Christ Jesus for good works, which God prepared beforehand, that we should walk in them.

Figured

I finally figured it out!
I now know my role in life.
I now know my gifts.
My spirit's in lift,
And I feel so good I could shout!

I no longer fret over failure.
I'm proud just to get out and try.
For failure is feedback of what not to do,
And I will not stop till I break through.
I finally figured it out!

I will not be held back.
Nor will I worry over traits I lack.
I will continue to push ahead
And concentrate on my talents instead.
I finally figured it out!

I wish to be strong more than rich;
True strength of character is what I wish.
To serve and assist those in need—
Now, that is a goal I hope to achieve.
I finally figured it out!

I finally know what I need:
Strong faith, good health, a loving mate—yes, indeed.
I finally appreciate what I have:
Strong faith, good health, a loving mate. Don't you see?
I finally figured it out!

So what is it that's making you frown?
Is that fear that keeps on slowing you down?
What is it that you really want?
Can you write out the goals you desire in large font?
Wouldn't you one day love to shout?
Then all you must do … is figure it out!

Deuteronomy 28:12 (KJV)

The LORD shall open unto thee his good treasure, the heaven to give the rain unto thy land in his season, and to bless all the work of thine hand: and thou shalt lend unto many nations, and thou shalt not borrow.

Success

Ah, success. What an aphrodisiac.
Intoxicating and invigorating,
And that's a natural fact.

Success leads to the goal of even more success,
For once you excel, it's hard to settle for less,
Especially if you've been blessed.

Success is one of the world's greatest deodorants,
For no matter how many times you fail,
Just keep getting up; one huge success, and you get over it,
and again set sail.

Success is also the best revenge.
Don't get mad—get successful.
It feels really good, and it is no sin,
And at night your sleep will be restful.

Don't look for success at the expense of others.
This world is plentiful. Why take from one another?
Just do what God has led you to do,
And your big moment will come shining through.

But be careful that success doesn't change who you are,
For failure is the mirror image, and is never away very far.
Be humble in your success and try to serve others.
Try not to be selfish, and keep good fortune under cover.

For when the day that your bell tolls for the final time,
You can look back with pride and say, "I shared mine!"
Grace bought me this success, and that's a God-given fact.
Ah, yes, success—what an aphrodisiac!

Isaiah 40:31 (KJV)

But they that wait upon the Lord shall renew their strength.

Affirmation

Sometimes I'll fail, yet I'll succeed.
My best help comes when I'm on my knees.

I may be slowed, but never stopped.
My only goal is to reach the top.

For as sure as God gives me grace,
I will continue to run this race.

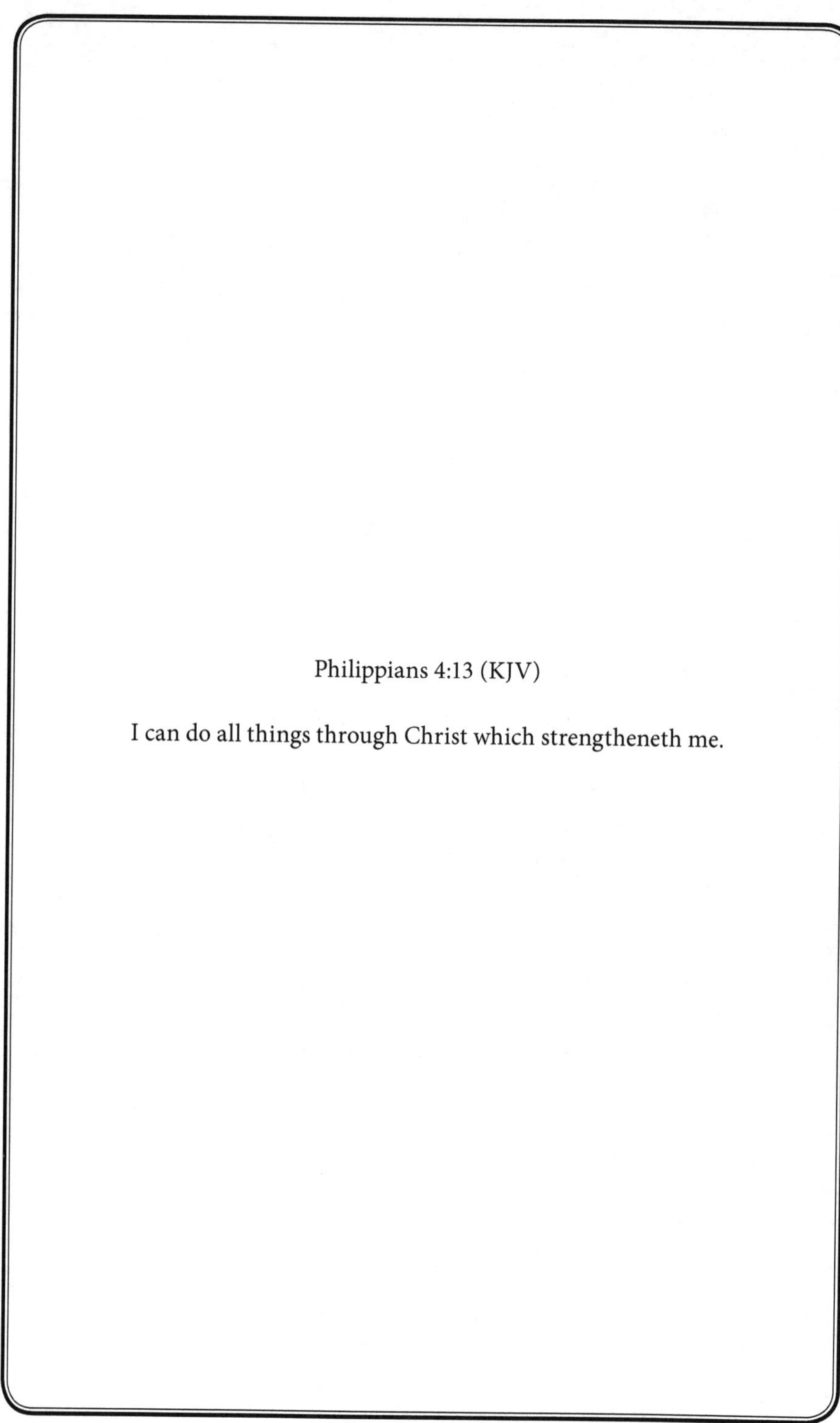

Philippians 4:13 (KJV)

I can do all things through Christ which strengtheneth me.

Try

I'd rather try and fail,
Than to sit and wail.
Yes, I'd take that any day of the week.
For to try and fail takes inner strength,
Whereas wailing is the way out for the weak.

I'd rather choose and lose, even if I look like a fool,
Than not choose as the world passes me by.
Because winners keep trying while losers keep whining
Such a wasted life until they die.

Sometimes friends and family too will try to stop you
From reaching and obtaining your goal.
Because misery loves company,
They don't want you to succeed, truth be told.

If you succeed, you leave while they're still in their rut,
Growing more and more bitter each day.
All your failures before mean nothing anymore.
"You're just lucky" is what they say.

Don't let the ridicule of others stop your drive.
Don't let setbacks end your dreams.
With positive attitude and undying faith,
You can overcome failure and schemes.

Know that failure is not final; it's just feedback.
I was told that, and I believe
If God led me to it, He'll take me through it.
Keep the faith, and He'll help you to succeed.

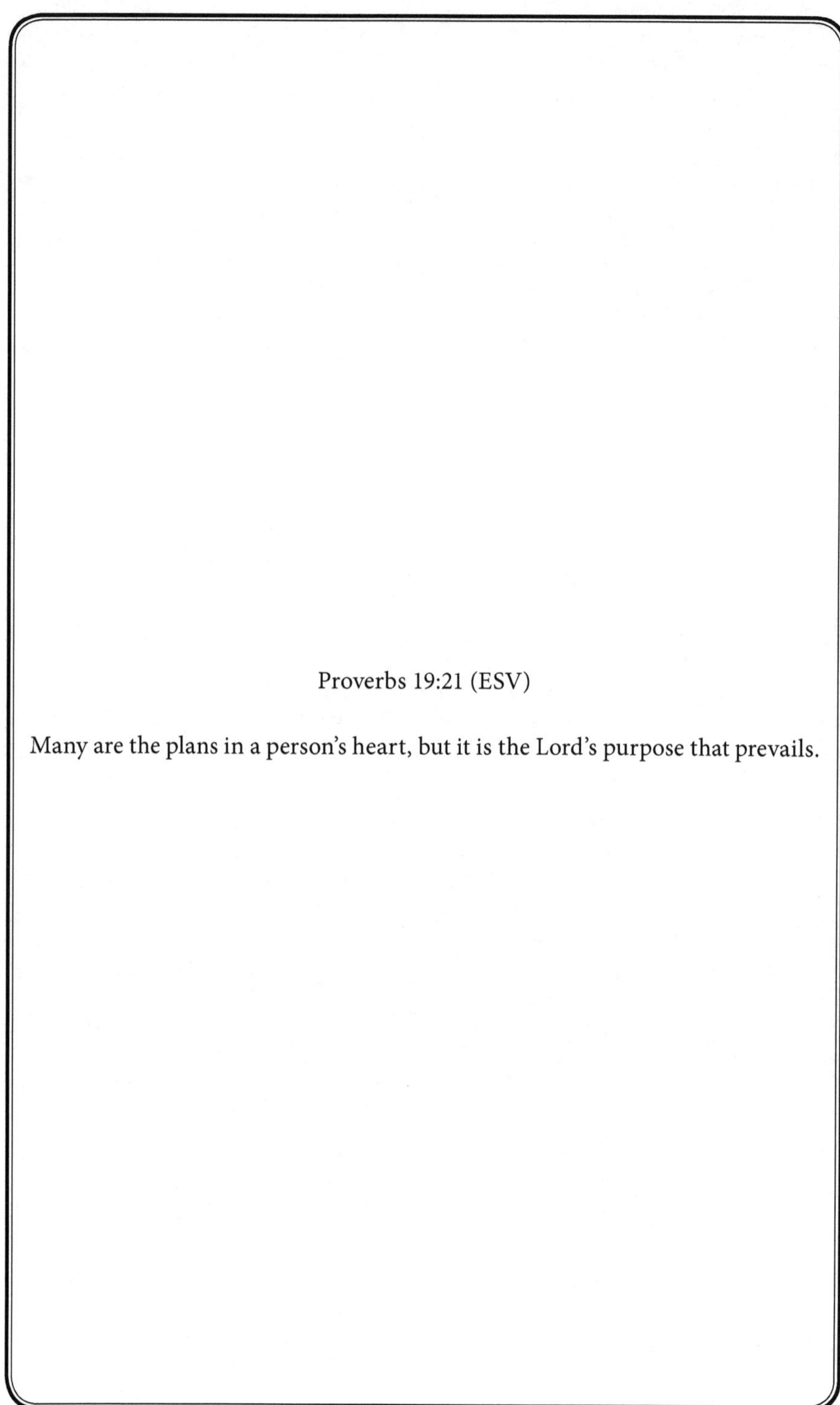

Proverbs 19:21 (ESV)

Many are the plans in a person's heart, but it is the Lord's purpose that prevails.

Purpose

Are you here to do something?
Or are you here for something to do?
God has put purpose in each of our lives.
Discovering your purpose is up to you.

Have you looked at the many pieces in your life,
And tried to bring a defined sense of order?
Written down what you have versus what you want?
Or is your answer a very vague "Sort of ..."

You talk yourself out of things faster than into them;
Other things you do on a whim.
Your mind is often filled with ridicule and doubt,
Some things you constantly worry about.

One minute you're absolutely sure this thing is going to work;
Then you're sad, and your feelings are hurt.
Next you wonder, *What could I have been thinking about?*
And from the world you just want to get out.

The seed of purpose is buried deep, to keep the roots strong,
But it will never flourish until the gardener comes along.
Find your purpose, nourish it, and then just watch it grow.
God designed it just for you, so let the whole world know.

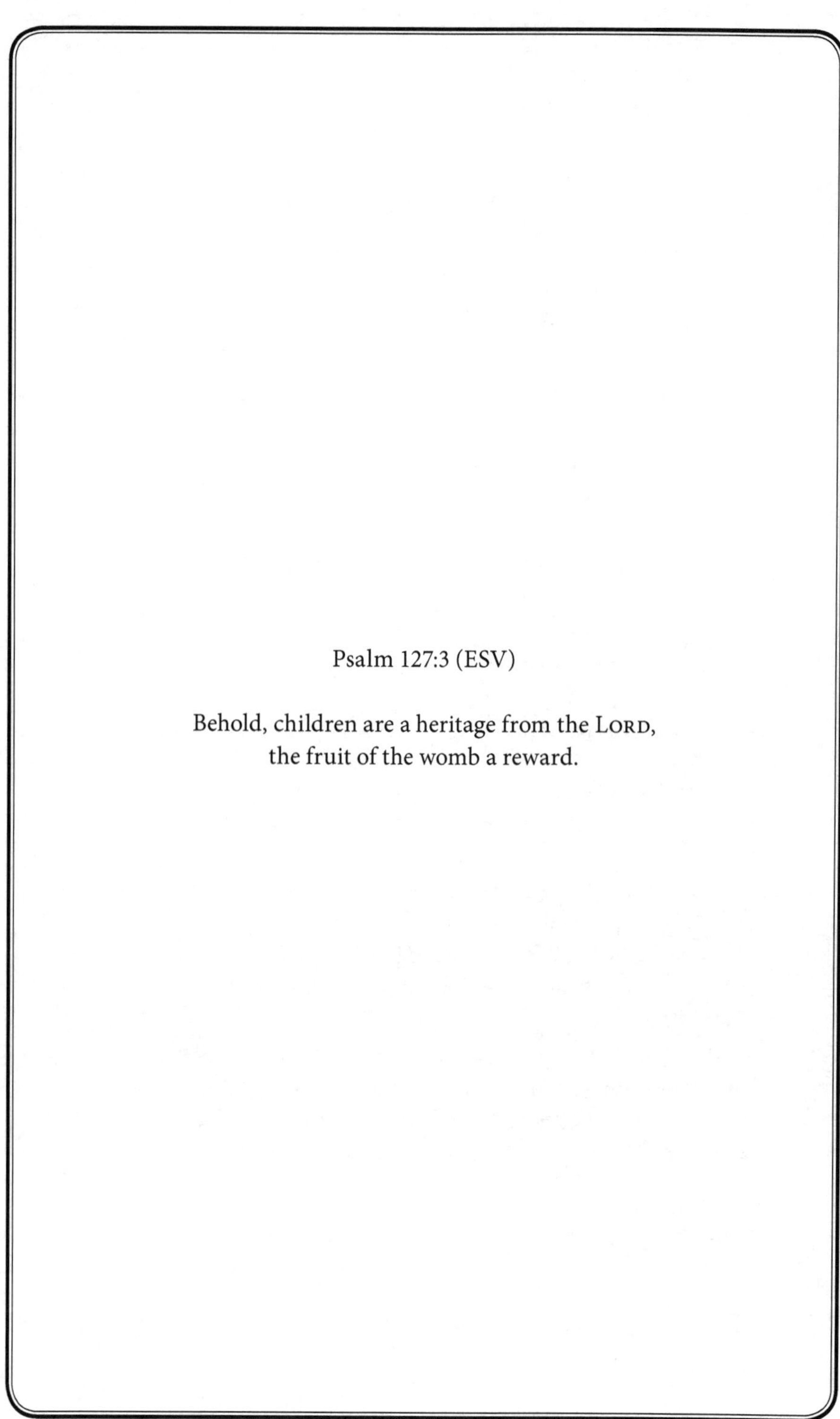

Psalm 127:3 (ESV)

Behold, children are a heritage from the Lord,
the fruit of the womb a reward.

Don't Make the Child Choose

It's a story that's been told,
And I know it's very old.
But in this case it's worth telling once again
About two who used to win
As both lovers and as friends.

But now it seems their broken hearts
They just can't mend.
It's a love that didn't last,
And a marriage that's now past.

And these two think they're the only ones concerned,
And now a powerful lesson they all must learn:
They forgot about the kid,
And all the harm their fighting did.

Harsh words between those two
Hit the child's ears too.
Sometimes a word can hit as hard as a fist,
As the child was use to seeing things end with a kiss.

So now she's torn between mom and dad,
And the love the family had.
Don't make the child choose;
Either way she's going to lose.

All she's ever known is you two being one.
For her to have to pick
Makes her feel she's being tricked.
In the middle of your fight—that's not right.

If you continue to be bitter,
Both your hearts are going to wither,
And the child will become confused and drift away.
If you're not sure of what to do,
Call on God to see you through.
Don't delay—talk to Him right now, today!

1 Peter 4:10 (NIV)

Each of you should use whatever gift you have received to serve others, as faithful stewards of God's grace in its various forms.

Service

We seem to have a problem with service
And forget that the point is to serve.
But when we find service demeaning,
We should take a look in the Word.

Jesus came here to serve us,
Yet we feel we're too good to serve others.
How can it be wrong, and why can't we get along
With those we should call our brothers?

If we can't have a spirit of giving
But always look to receive,
How can we possibly expect God's blessings
At night when we fall to our knees?

Most women are better than men
At serving, and caring, and such.
But today that attitude seems to be changing,
And many don't care near as much.

There is great honor in serving,
Especially if you have been blessed to give.
For one day you may need service from others,
Depending on how long you live.

In the twilight of your days on earth,
When you look back on all you have served,
It's good to know you'll be blessed from above
With the rest you so richly deserve.

Galatians 6:10 (ESV)

So then, as we have opportunity, let us do good to everyone, and especially to those who are of the household of faith.

Responsibility

What are you responsible for?
Who are you responsible to?
What are others waiting for?
Who is depending on you?

What abilities do you possess?
Who are you taking care of?
Do you respond to friends and strangers,
Or just to the ones you love?

Those who have the ability
Are often obliged to respond.
For to have it and not use it
Is simply to abuse it,
And that should never be done.

Ability is truly a blessing,
But the response part is up to you.
For what we don't use, we often lose,
And blessings are not ours to choose.

So what have been your responses
To the blessings you have been given?
Have your abilities blessed someone else
Through the spirit of how you're living?

Your blessings cost you nothing;
God gave them to you free.
To recognize and give back to others
Is your responsibility.

I realize that you are young
And don't understand where I'm coming from.
I thought that I'd write it all down
So you could look back and become.

God will send you someone;
Satan will send many too.
The influences you decide to follow
Are totally up to you.

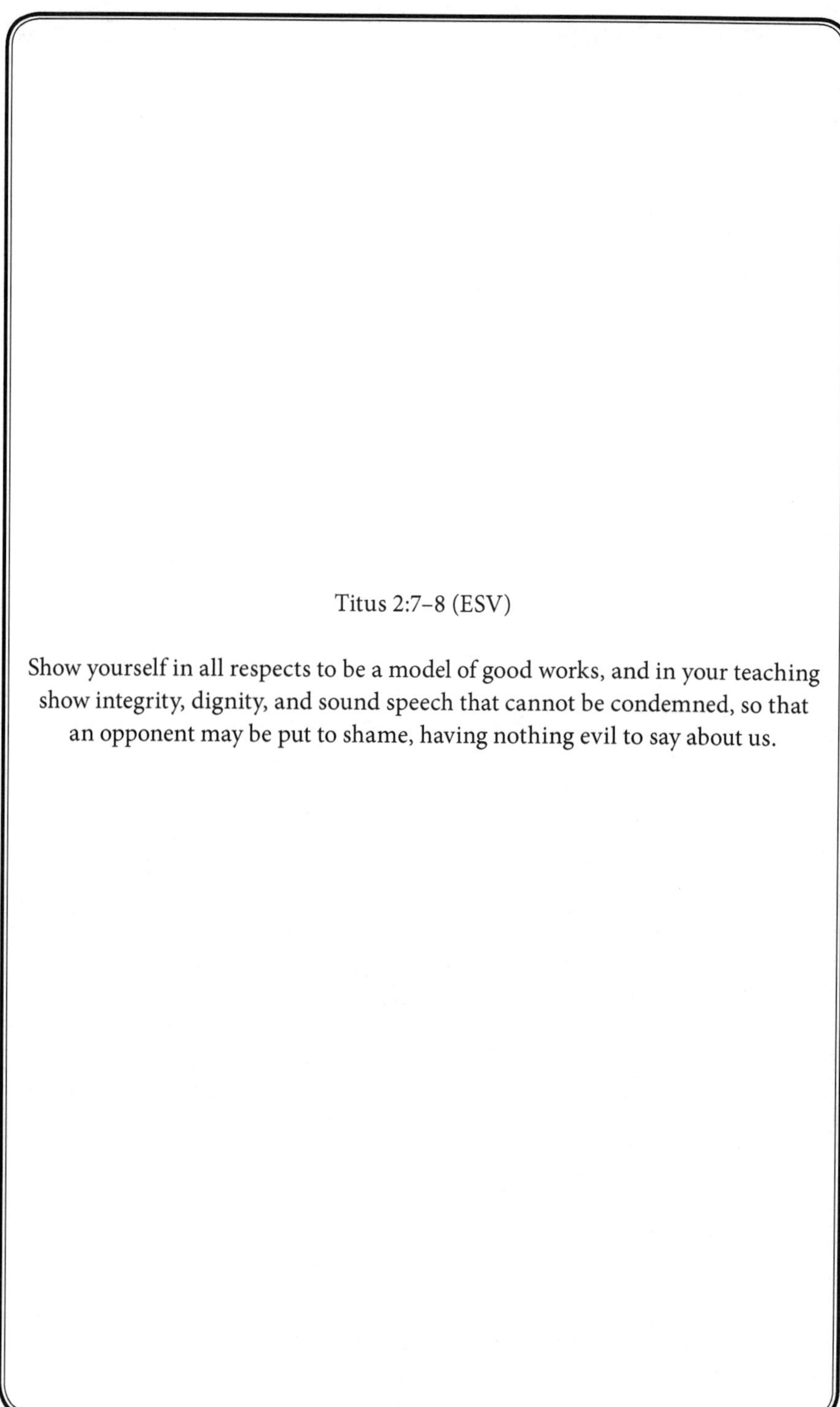

Titus 2:7–8 (ESV)

Show yourself in all respects to be a model of good works, and in your teaching show integrity, dignity, and sound speech that cannot be condemned, so that an opponent may be put to shame, having nothing evil to say about us.

Influence

Influence can come in many shapes, sometimes in different styles.
It can take place all of a sudden, or it may take a while.
It may come from a top educator, or the innocent lips of a child.
Someone composed, calm, and collected, or someone totally wild.

Influence can sway you from this way to that.
It can knock you down or bring you back.
It can change your thought and character too.
There are really no limits to what influence can do.

It can heal the hurt or cause the pain.
It plays a conscious or unconscious game.
Influence may be known or unknown; this is true.
You may not realize what it does to you.

But others may see, from the outside looking in,
The influence of strangers, lovers, or friends.
The way you act, the things you do
Reveal the influence they have on you.

Just be aware that this is true,
Not all influences are good for you.
Surround yourself with people of character,
And you'll be blessed with things that matter.

Proverbs 16:9 (ESV)

The heart of man plans his way, but the Lord establishes his steps.

Be Encouraged

In order to get ahead, look inside your heart,
For the hardest part of getting ahead
Is knowing where to start.

Once you get your goal in place,
It's easy to set your sight.
To obtaining milestones one at a time,
You're sure to get it right.

Proverbs 15:13 (NIV)

A happy heart makes the face cheerful, but heartache crushes the spirit.

You Don't Have to Tell It

You don't have to tell it;
It shows on your face.
Whether you're winning or losing
Is not as important as running the race.

If you are pulling ahead and beginning to find success,
Your knees begin buckling from the oncoming stress.
Seeking self-improvement through numerous outside sources,
Or totally unconcerned with many of your life choices.

You don't have to tell it;
It shows on your face.

If your friends and acquaintances have an uplifting spirit,
Or only negative feedback from them every time you hear it;
If your family is supportive of all your goals and dreams,
Or simply hold you back with their negativity and schemes.

If your spiritual spirit is not as strong as it should be,
And the demons of life just won't seem to set you free,
Then a positive influence changes your whole attitude,
And through a renewed will, you just refuse to lose.

You don't have to tell it;
It shows on your face.

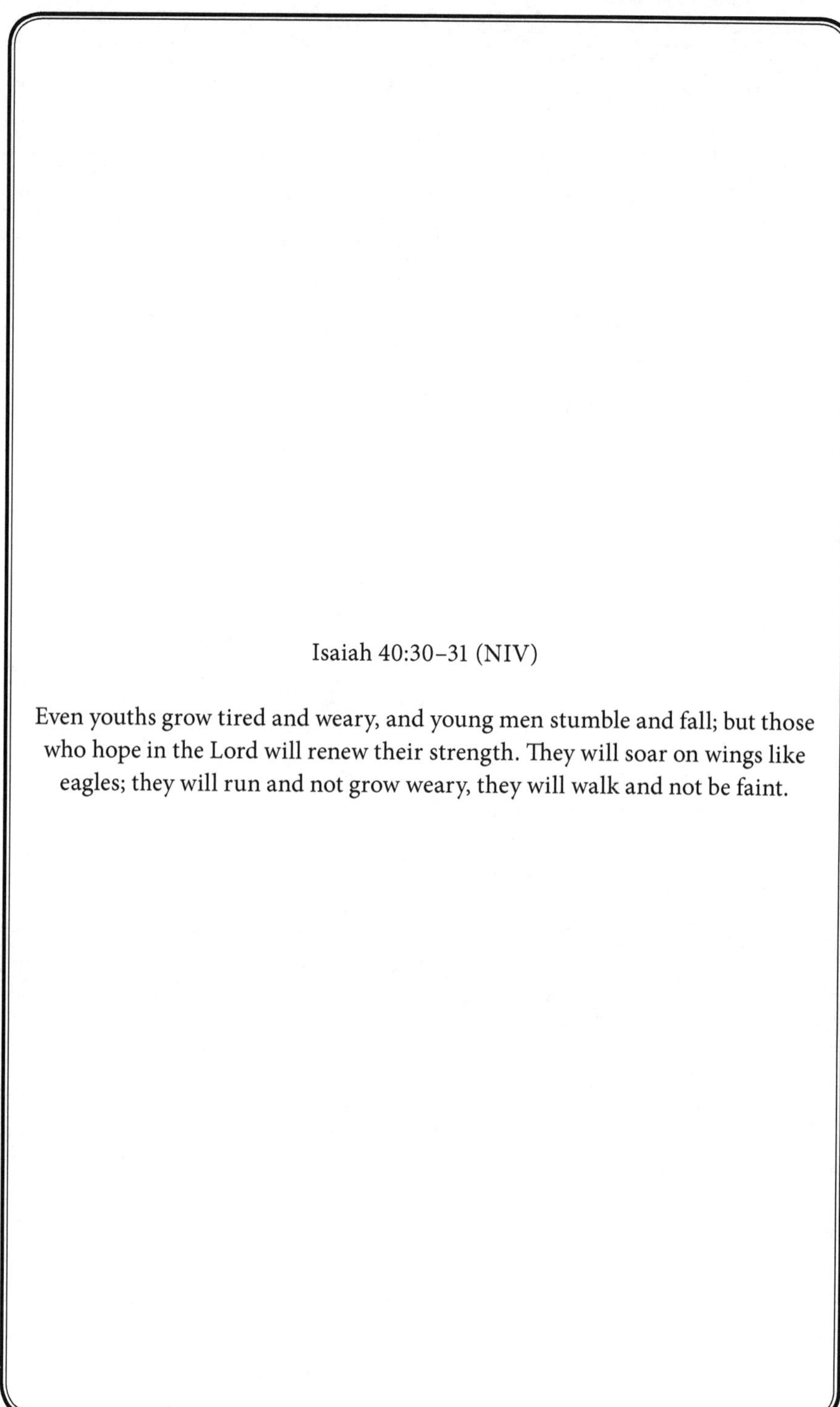

Isaiah 40:30–31 (NIV)

Even youths grow tired and weary, and young men stumble and fall; but those who hope in the Lord will renew their strength. They will soar on wings like eagles; they will run and not grow weary, they will walk and not be faint.

How Far

How far are you willing to go?
What seeds are you trying to sow?
What lessons in life have you learned?
What bridges do you regret that you've burned?

Who has made a difference in your life?
Whose life have you touched in return?
Were the experiences of a positive nature?
Or were the roads full of twist and turns?

Do you focus more on the journey ahead?
Or does the destination fire your desires instead?
When you lose, do you grow from the lesson,
Or turn bitter to the point of depression?

Are you willing to go the extra mile?
When the road you are on gets rough,
Can you dig in, get fixed on the win?
Can you stay focused when times get tough?

How far are you willing to go?
It takes more than just skill, you should know.
If you're willing to try, to the point where you'd die,
Then you're willing to go much further than you know.

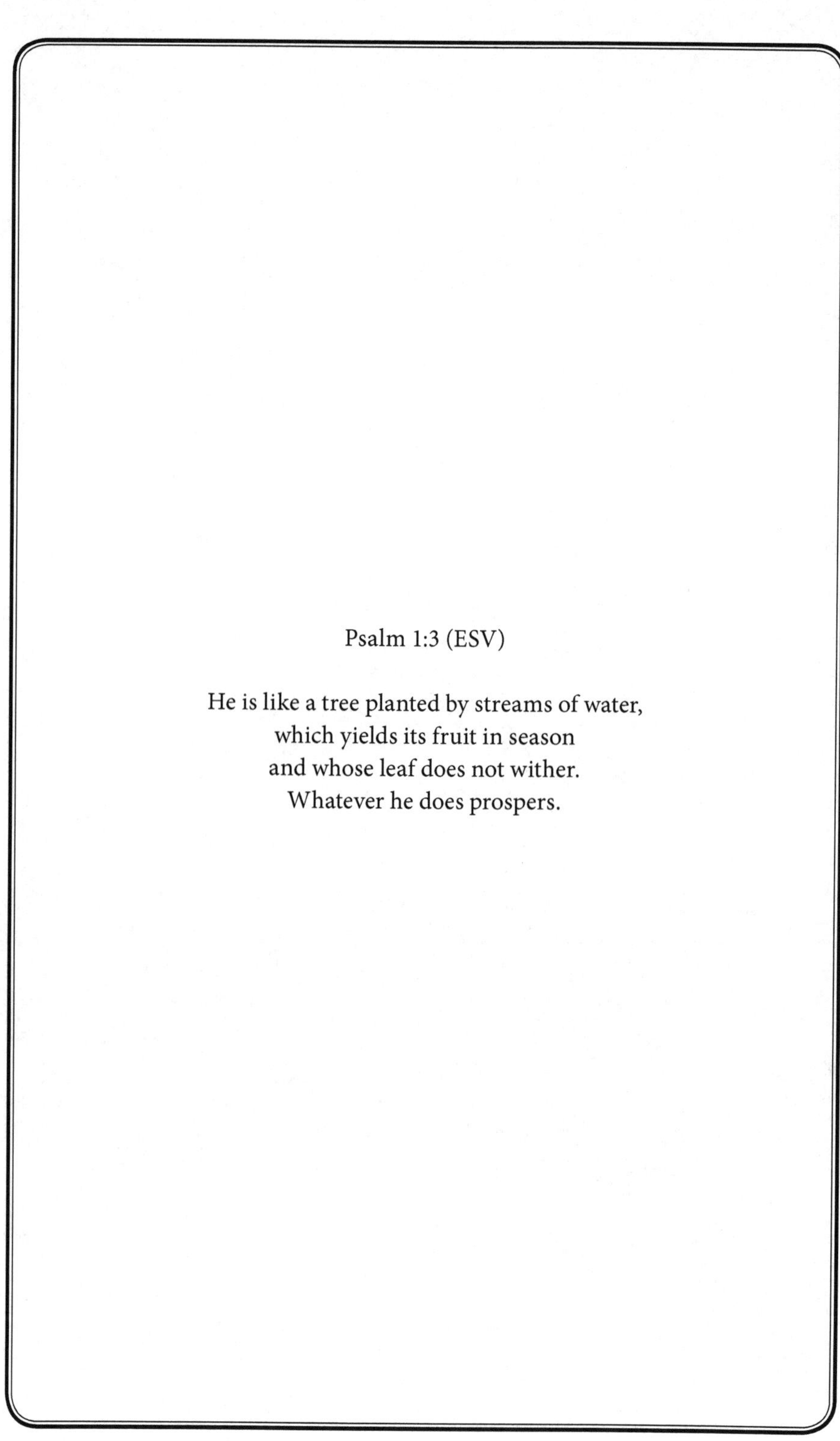

Psalm 1:3 (ESV)

He is like a tree planted by streams of water,
which yields its fruit in season
and whose leaf does not wither.
Whatever he does prospers.

Reflections

What is the true measure of success?
Is it how much you have, or just doing your best?
Who decides how much is enough?
Do you work from a plan, or just right off the cuff?

Who rules on what's good and what is bad?
What keeps you happy, and what makes you sad?
What is it that most people think they really need?
Is it for them to win or for you to concede?

Just how far is going too far?
Is it the distance you run, or drive in a car?
Is love more important, or is it money?
Which one works for you? Isn't life funny?

Is it better to be married or to be single?
Have a life companion or continue to mingle?
Is it better to be a loner or have friends?
Do you look forward to beginnings, or hope for the end?

It is your life, and you have a choice.
You can remain silent or lift up your voice.
If you check, you'll find it's all in your attitude.
You decide, today: Do you win or lose?

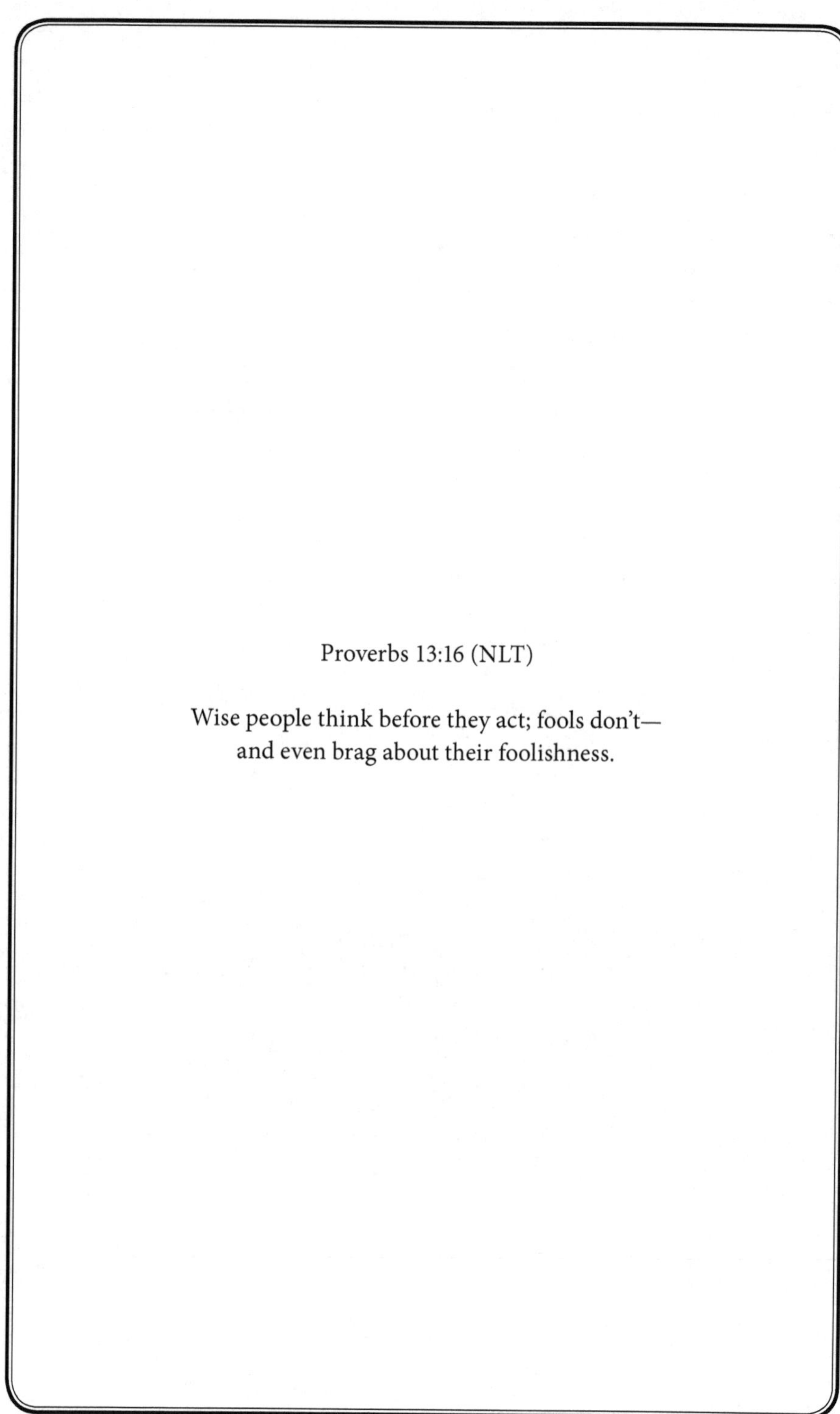

Proverbs 13:16 (NLT)

Wise people think before they act; fools don't—
and even brag about their foolishness.

Stop

"Stop to think" I've often heard
But never quite understood.
If I stopped to think instead of react,
How could that do me much good?

It took a while to understand
The value of a pause.
For if I stopped to think a bit,
I'd understand the cause.

Reacting without thinking often has a consequence
And gives others looking on the impression you have no sense.
Sometimes it's wise to take a breath, just a moment to exhale.
A simple pause can make the difference of whether you succeed or fail.

Stop to think—that's good advice.
I think I'd better listen.
For if I react too soon and fail,
I know I'll be here wishing.

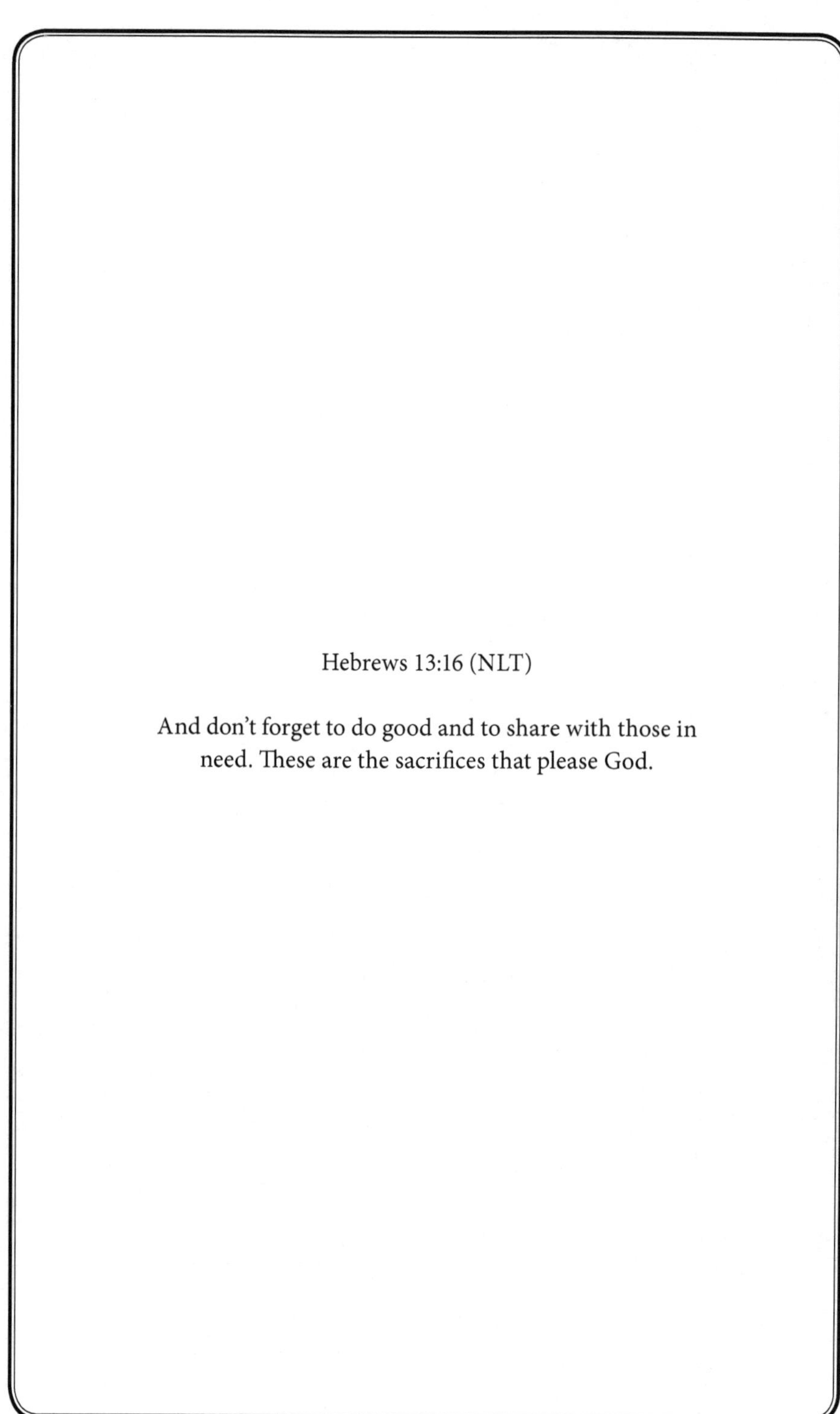

Hebrews 13:16 (NLT)

And don't forget to do good and to share with those in need. These are the sacrifices that please God.

Who

Who are you?
What personal identity do you prescribe to?
Of course you know who you think you are,
But do you know just who they think you are?

When you look in the mirror,
You know who you see.
But what about the rumors
They take you to be?

How do you prove you are you?
What is it you have to do
To prove you're not the you they're thinking about?
What will it take for you to remove that doubt?

Talking the talk is important, that's very true.
But people will believe even more in what you do.
So if what they think is important to you,
Then be very aware of what you do.

For your character is what they use to describe you;
Your actions are the things that truly define you.
So if you want them to see you as you think you are,
Then you must become the you that they see you are.

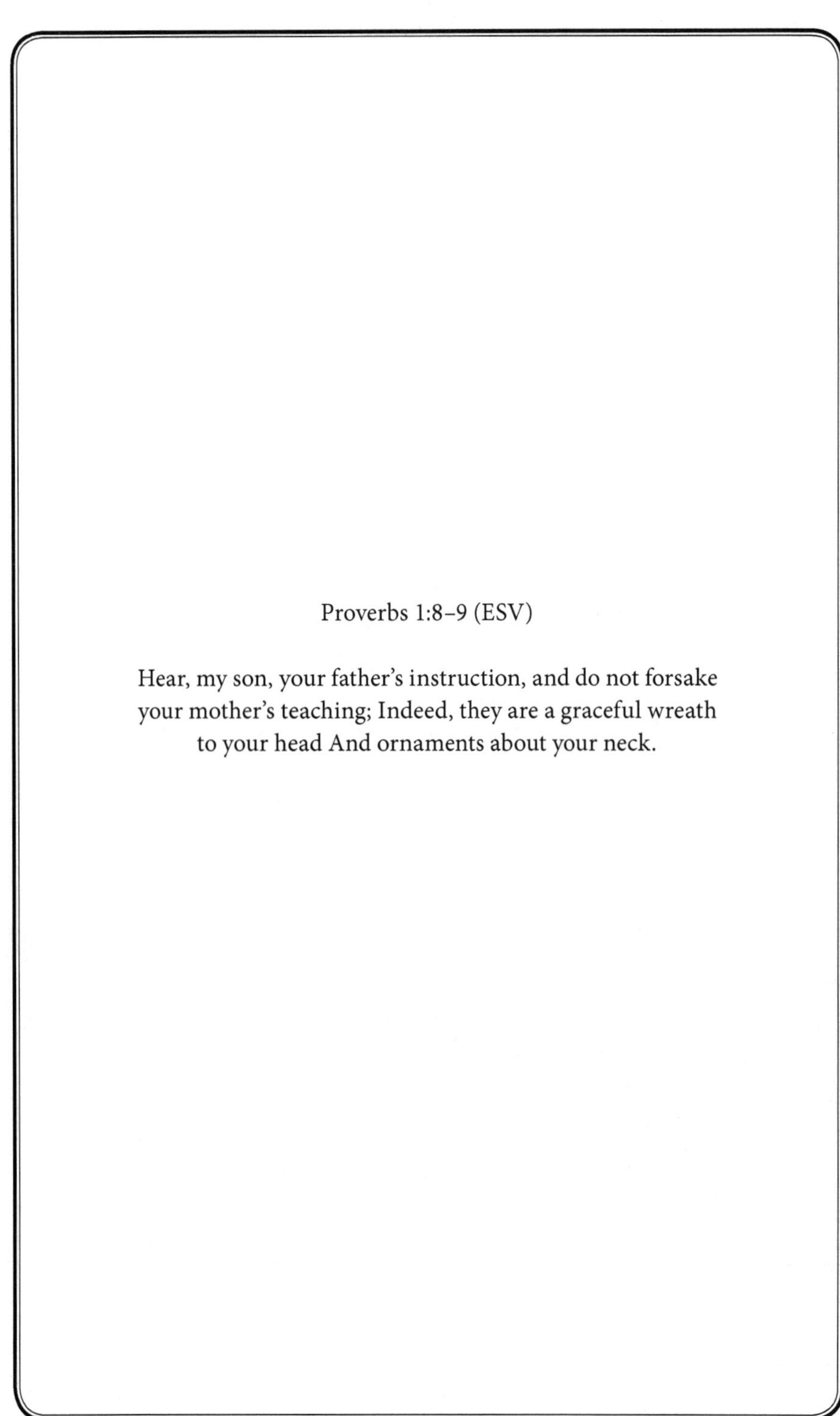

Proverbs 1:8–9 (ESV)

Hear, my son, your father's instruction, and do not forsake your mother's teaching; Indeed, they are a graceful wreath to your head And ornaments about your neck.

Youth

The times of our youth are not easy.
Not all that we do will be pleasing.
To be prepared for life at all times,
Sometimes I don't get the reason.

"Pray up daily; be on high alert"
Is what I hear the pastor extol.
But being with friends and getting a little wild?
Now, that's what's burning deep in my soul.

"Keep your guard up; there's danger out there"
Is my mother's constant warning.
What can be so wrong with being with friends
Till night gives way to morning?

"Be not afraid; you'll soon be a man"
Is what I so often hear.
But how am I ever to grow to manhood
If they insist on keeping me near?

Some lessons just can't be taught;
Many lessons can only be learned.
So let me make my mistakes as I grow.
I appreciate all your concern.

Galatians 5:17 (KJV)

For the flesh lusteth against the Spirit, and the Spirit against the flesh: and these are contrary the one to the other: so that ye cannot do the things that ye would.

Proverbs 16:9 (KJV)

A man's heart deviseth his way: but the LORD directeth his steps.

Why Do We?

Why do we all envy people
For the wrong things or the wrong reasons,
When we have been promised that if we are patient,
We all have a due season?

Why do we act so surprised
When we encounter things in life?
The hard times make us stronger
And more appreciative of the things that go right.

Why do we not recognize
We all need encouragement?
True strength doesn't always come from within;
Sometimes it's heaven sent.

Why do we not understand
We will be compelled to do wrong?
To recognize and repent
Will increase our faith and make us strong.

Why do we always find it easier
To destroy than to create,
When creation establishes a legacy
For others to emulate?

Why do we all like to think
That we must be the one,
When the One was sent to save us all,
And before Him there can be none?

Why do we not simply enjoy
The blessings of this earth?
For He has ordered our every step
Since long before our birth.

Why do we ...?

James 1:23–25 (ESV)

For if anyone is a hearer of the word and not a doer, he is like a man who looks intently at his natural face in a mirror. For he looks at himself and goes away and at once forgets what he was like. But the one who looks into the perfect law, the law of liberty, and perseveres, being no hearer who forgets but a doer who acts, he will be blessed in his doing.

Something Is Holding Me Back

It seems sometimes for every forward step,
I find myself three steps back.
I try forcing myself to get ahead,
But life knocks me down instead.

It's got to be the hand of faith,
Not from talents that I lack.
Something is holding me back.
Could it possibly be the way I act?

I do my best to get good grades,
But the teachers conspire against me.
When I go to play on my favorite team,
They say I'm all about me, rather than we.

No one seems to understand.
Why is it so hard to see?
Something is holding me back.
Could it possibly be the way I act?

For a moment I thought, *Maybe it's me*,
But soon that thought was gone.
I know that I am right on point.
Others just wish me harm.

I don't know what's wrong with them.
Why can't they just see the facts?
Something is holding me back.
Could it possibly be … the way I act?

Deuteronomy 20:4 (NIV)

For the LORD your God is the one who goes with you to fight for you against your enemies to give you victory.

Victim or Victor

Victim or victor is truly a matter of choice.
You can be a victim by simply not raising your voice.

If you choose to be a victor, preparations must be made.
Victims leave life to chance and never make the grade.

Victors know that they must change, and even change again.
Victims get run over in life; they don't prepare as marksmen.

Victims find many folks to blame—everyone but themselves.
Victors maximize their potential and rise from the depths of hell.

Victors don't entertain self-pity, no time for it at all.
Victims complain when times are hard and wonder whom they can call.

Descartes says, "I think; therefore I am," and victors are like that too.
Victims cry, "Why always me? why couldn't that happen to you?"

Victim or victor—you decide; the choice is in your hands.
Sit idly by and be victimized, or be a victor and take a stand.

Romans 10:8–9 (KJV)

That if thou shalt confess with thy mouth the Lord Jesus, and shalt believe in thine heart that God hath raised him from the dead, thou shalt be saved. For with the heart man believeth unto righteousness; and with the mouth confession is made unto salvation.

Do It Now

If you're going to do it, do it now.
Why ever would you wait?
Opportunity is always lost
By those who hesitate.

Do it now; the idea is fresh.
Enthusiasm is really high.
Your energy now is truly flowing.
Don't let time pass you by.

Ecclesiastes 10:10 (KJV)

If the iron is blunt, and one does not sharpen the edge, he must use more strength, but wisdom helps one to succeed.

Is It Worth It?

How far are you willing to go?
What seeds are you willing to sow?
How much of yourself are you willing to invest?
What excites the heart beating within your breast?

What are you willing to sacrifice?
How drastically are you willing to reshape your life?
How long are you willing to stick it out
When times get so hard you want to scream and shout?

Can you handle failing without being a failure?
Continue to fight for goals, whether minor or major.
What are you willing to learn?
Some technology or process for which you still yearn.

What are you willing to unlearn?
Some old habits you have that may yet get you burned.
Just who are you willing to trust?
Are you willing to cooperate in a mutual brain thrust?

What relationships are you willing to build?
Are you willing to allow others to showcase their skills?
What relationships are you willing to break?
Can you let some go if your goal's at stake?

How much is it really worth to you?
Is it truly a dream you want to come true?
Have you really thought this through,
To determine just what it's all worth to you?

Deuteronomy 6:5–9 (NET)

You must love the Lord your God with your whole mind, your whole being, and all your strength. These words I am commanding you today must be kept in mind, and you must teach them to your children and speak of them as you sit in your house, as you walk along the road, as you lie down, and as you get up. You should tie them as a reminder on your forearm and fasten them as symbols on your forehead. Inscribe them on the doorframes of your houses and gates.

Dear Black Man

Dear black man,
When will you take your stand?
Your woman and your child are waiting.
Will you extend your hand?

Will you take responsibility
For the child you two have made?
Or will you simply cut and run
When you know you should have stayed?

Can you be the man your woman needs
When hard times come around?
Or disappear like a puff of smoke,
Just nowhere to be found?

Can you truly be a dad
To that child that you have fathered?
Or is fatherhood too much for you,
And you just can't be bothered?

Do you realize how much you're needed
Throughout the black neighborhood?
To see you as a positive model
Would do us all much good.

This may seem a lot of pressure
Just being a black man.
So much of the past to overcome
With flames of hope to fan.

It may be unfair to do,
Life putting so much on you.
But be strong and honorable, black man.
We need you to pull us through!

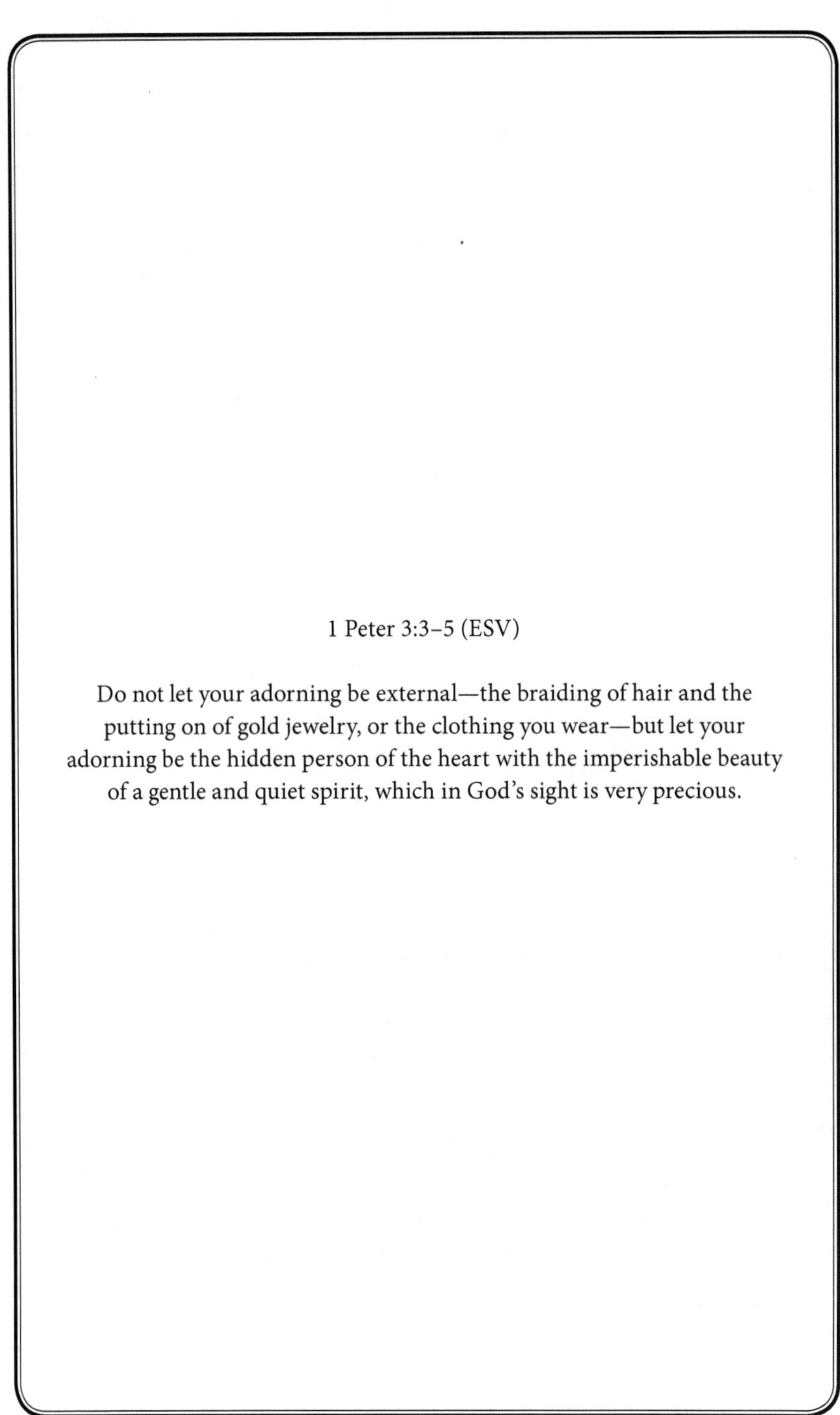

1 Peter 3:3–5 (ESV)

Do not let your adorning be external—the braiding of hair and the putting on of gold jewelry, or the clothing you wear—but let your adorning be the hidden person of the heart with the imperishable beauty of a gentle and quiet spirit, which in God's sight is very precious.

Dear Sister Black

Dear sister black,
What is it you want out of life?
To be a woman, lover, mother,
Or maybe even a wife?

To have an education,
A good job and folks respect?
To have a God you know and love,
And be relatively free from debt?

To have a family on whom you can depend?
To give support and understanding?
To provide you with alternative choices
And not be so demanding?

To have a man whom you can trust
To be yours and yours alone?
To go to work and share the load?
Whose love makes a happy home?

Well, you can have this, sister black.
Yes, all of this and more.
But the order in which you choose it
Is the method you must employ.

"Keep God first in all you do"
Is really sage advice.
Starting with Him as your foundation,
You're sure to get it right.

Be a woman; get educated
Before you become a mother.
Make sure the man is husband worthy
And not just merely a lover.

As for respect, you must first have it
Before you can receive.
How you carry yourself is important;
It is what others perceive.

My beautiful sister, you must remember
You carry the greatness seed.
You are meant for the heights of glory
Not to languish among the weeds.
So lift your face up to the sun
And carry yourself with pride.
Success in life is yours to choose.
God is on your side!

Proverbs 14:29 (ESV)

Whoever is slow to anger has great understanding, but
he who has a hasty temper exalts folly.

James 1:19–20 (ESV)

Know this, my beloved brothers: let every person be quick to hear, slow to speak, slow to anger; for the anger of man does not produce the righteousness of God.

Oh, Angry Black Child

Oh, angry black child, to whom are you speaking
In such a rude tone of voice?
Is there something in the way that you were raised
That makes you feel you have that choice?

Young angry black child, where did you learn
To speak with such disrespect?
You even dare to threaten others with acts of violence
If they try to put you in check.

Do you know, black child, what others have suffered
To provide the freedoms you enjoy?
To have you talk back, or even try to attack,
Are actions we simply deplore.

Just think, black child, where would you be
If parents really did just leave you alone?
You may think you're grown, but it's very doubtful
That you could truly make it on your own.

It seems, black child, that you think you are owed.
But what is it you are owed, and from whom?
If you don't turn away from this destructive path,
You are headed for certain doom.

Life is out there, black child, just waiting for you
To come out and get your part.
But your part must be earned, not taken or given,
And attitude is a great place to start.

Life is short, black child; don't waste it on anger,
When there's so much joy to be had.
You can give joy as well as receive;
To live without it is oh, so sad.

Proverbs 13:19 (NLT)

It is pleasant to see dreams come true, but fools refuse to turn from evil to attain them.

Ephesians 2:10 (ESV)

We are His workmanship, created in Christ Jesus for good works, which God prepared beforehand so that we would walk in them.

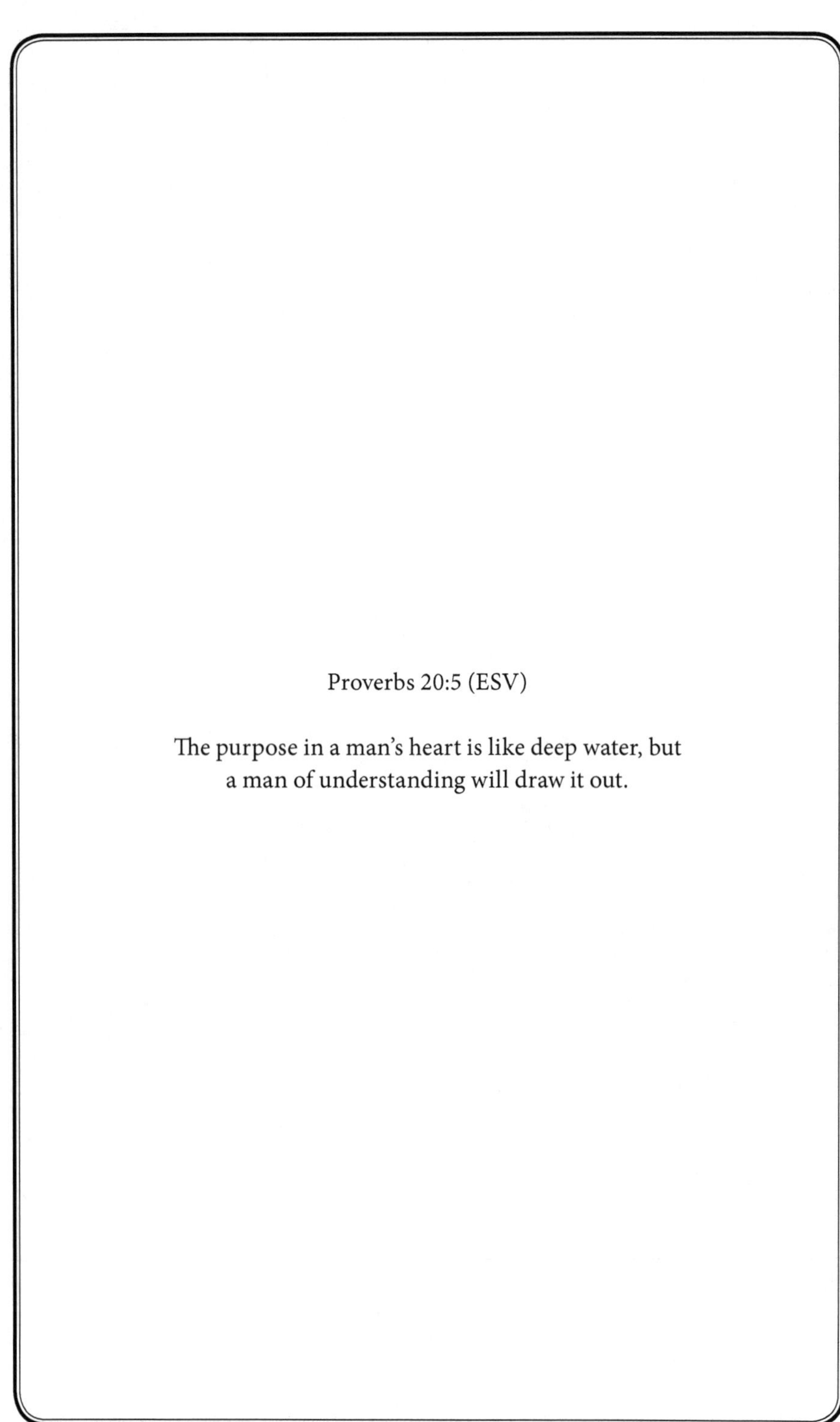

Proverbs 20:5 (ESV)

The purpose in a man's heart is like deep water, but a man of understanding will draw it out.

Do It

If you keep thinking about doing it, do it.
What is the worst that could happen?
Not doing at all is worse than failing;
Instead of living, you're just napping.

There's nothing wrong with having a dream,
But actions make dreams come true.
For once your dreams are laid out in plans,
Then comes the time to do.

Do it; if it's hard, you're on the right track,
For few things worth having come easy.
If it's on your mind like all the time,
Then it's time for you to get busy.

Do it; if it fails, do it again,
As many times as it takes.
For as often as you think of it,
Keep going until it works, for goodness' sakes.

Do it, whether friends support you or not.
True friends stay when you do it and fail.
False friends want only a share of your glory
For any success story they can tell.

Do it as long as the desire is burning
And the dream won't let you go.
To not do and look back at what might have been
Will truly hurt you so.

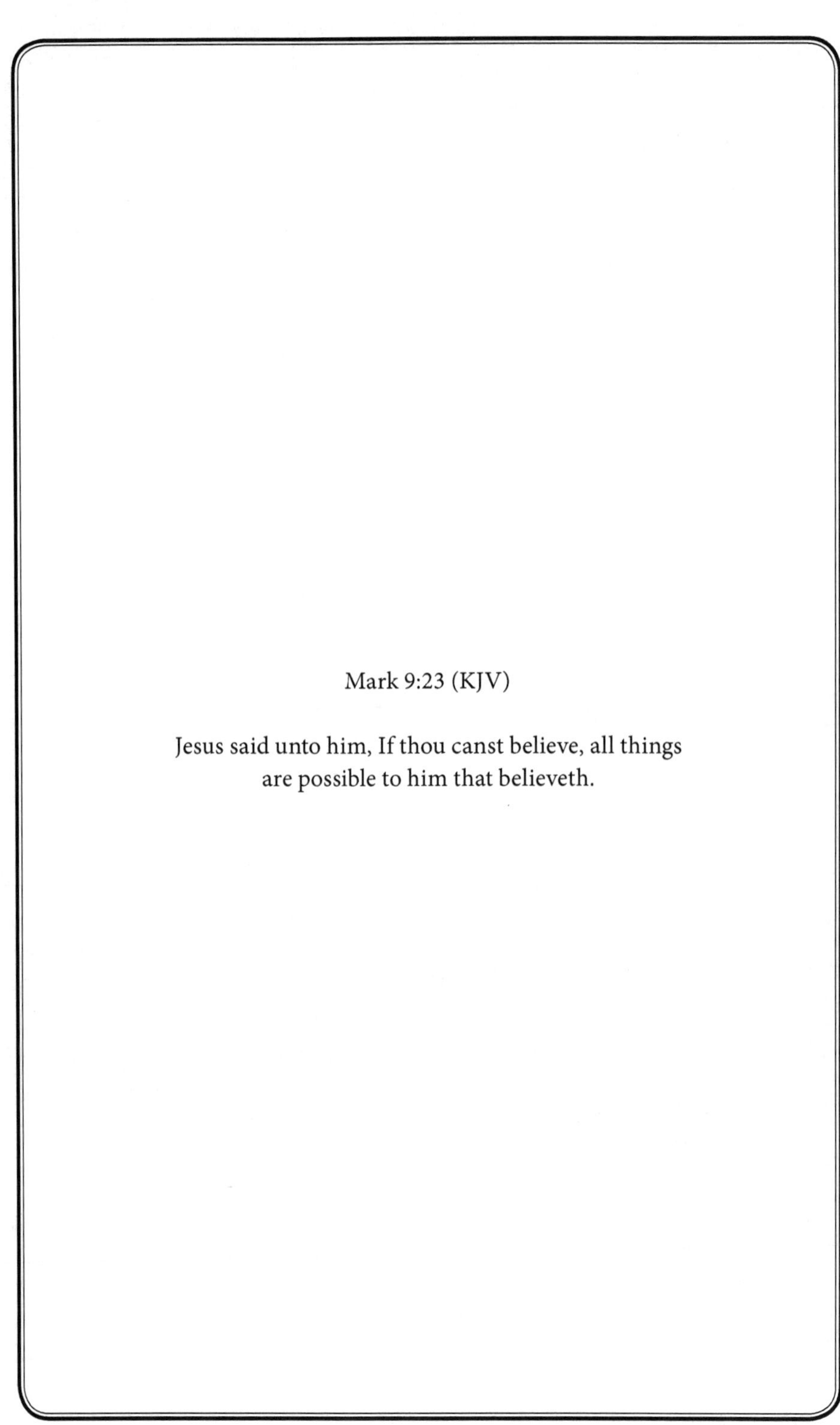

Mark 9:23 (KJV)

Jesus said unto him, If thou canst believe, all things are possible to him that believeth.

Goals and Dreams

Goals, dreams, sentimental things—
Maybe, maybe not.
These goals, these dreams, these sentimental things.
How many have you got?

From the mind, they spring like a living thing,
But the special ones flow from the heart.
The hardest thing about goals and dreams
Is knowing where to start.

If the dream is true, it possesses you
And commands your thoughts and deeds.
It's impossible to ignore the plan that's in store
And grows with every thought-seed.

Goals and dreams, maybe sentimental things,
But only if you fail to act.
So establish goals and follow your heart
Until the dream is a natural fact.

Proverbs 27:1(ESV)

Do not boast about tomorrow, For you do not know what a day may bring forth.

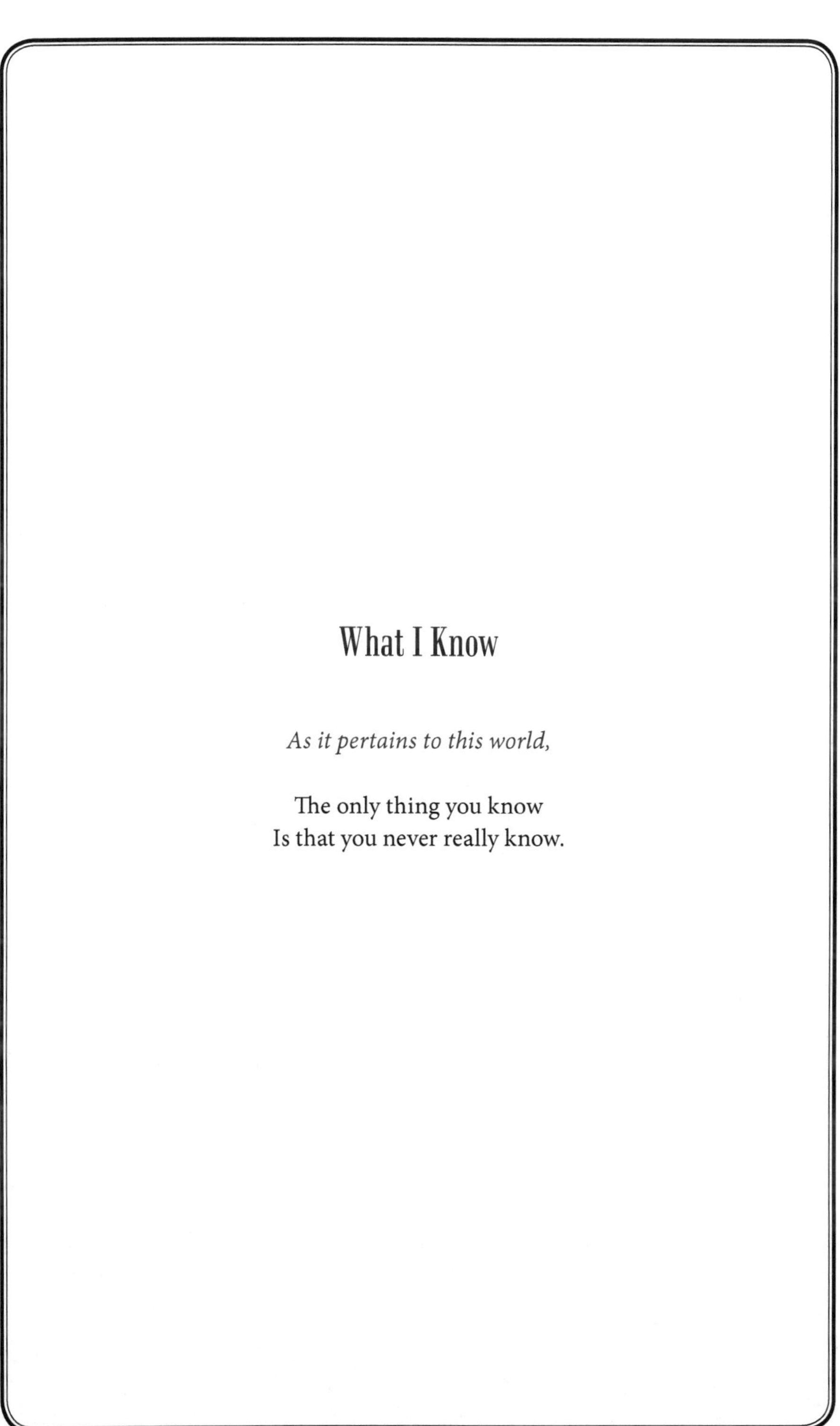

What I Know

As it pertains to this world,

The only thing you know
Is that you never really know.

Ecclesiastes 5:19 (KJV)

Every man also to whom God hath given riches and wealth, and hath given him power to eat thereof, and to take his portion, and to rejoice in his labour; this is the gift of God.

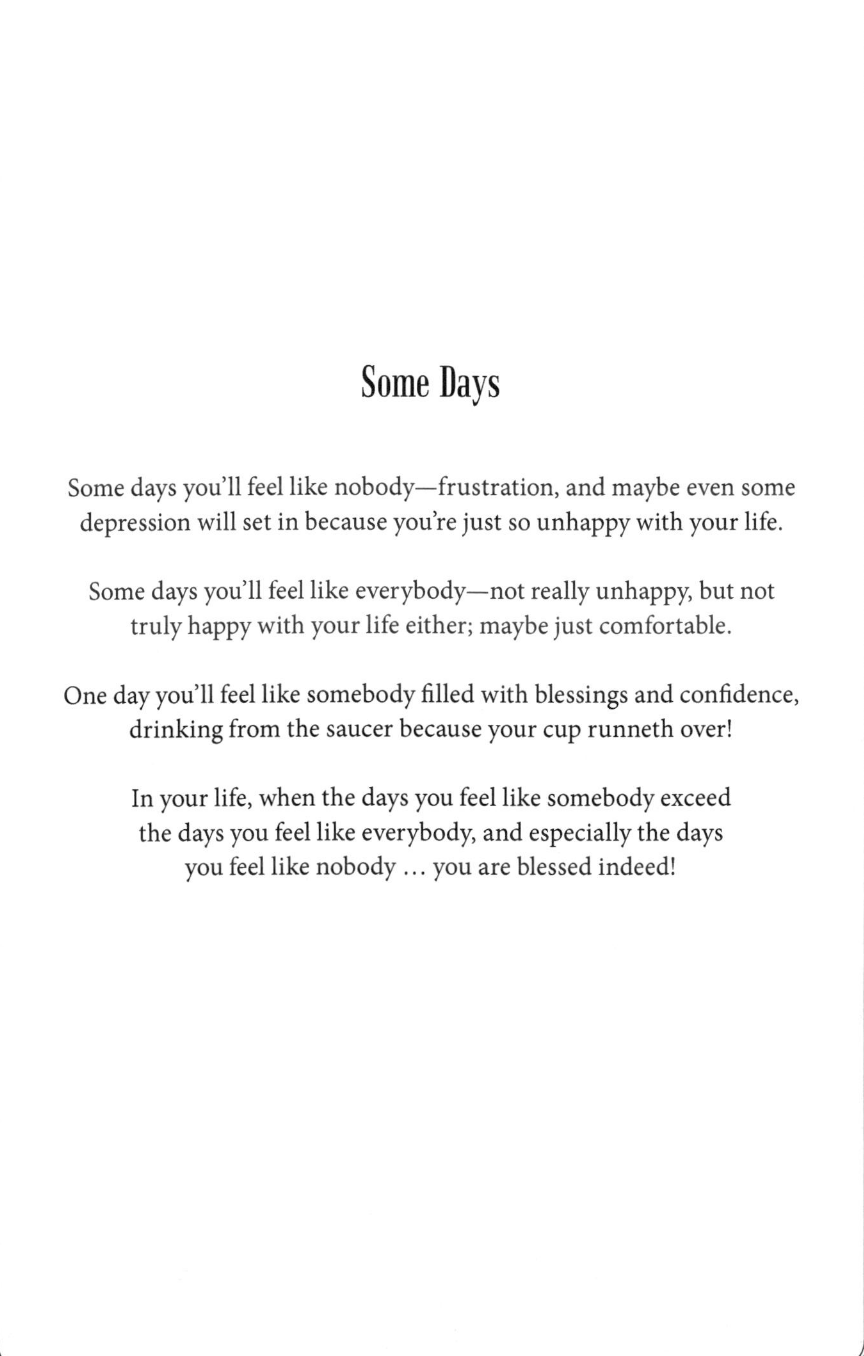

Some Days

Some days you'll feel like nobody—frustration, and maybe even some
depression will set in because you're just so unhappy with your life.

Some days you'll feel like everybody—not really unhappy, but not
truly happy with your life either; maybe just comfortable.

One day you'll feel like somebody filled with blessings and confidence,
drinking from the saucer because your cup runneth over!

In your life, when the days you feel like somebody exceed
the days you feel like everybody, and especially the days
you feel like nobody … you are blessed indeed!

Matthew 17:20 (ESV)

He said to them, "Because of your little faith. For truly, I say to you, if you have faith like a grain of mustard seed, you will say to this mountain, 'Move from here to there,' and it will move, and nothing will be impossible for you.

The Chase

Why do I continue to chase this dream?
Such an elusive thing.

One moment so clear, right in front of me,
Then vanished … or so it seems.

Philippians 4:8 (NLT)

And now, dear brothers and sisters, one final thing. Fix your thoughts on what is true, and honorable, and right, and pure, and lovely, and admirable. Think about things that are excellent and worthy of praise.

Metro Train Ride

I often wonder what your life is like.
Is it filled with joy, or pain?
I wonder what goes on inside your head
When I see you on the metro train.

No smile, no frown, no looking around;
No expression to reveal.
Just a longing glance through the train windows
At passing streets, cars, and hills.

The hustle and bustle of the rush-hour crowd
Does little to change your mood.
If you had the chance to change your life,
I wonder how you'd choose.

Do you have family, loved ones, and friends—
Someone whom you hold dear.
Are they near and close to you?
Do they bring you joy or tear?

And as you stare, mostly straight forward,
Never a word is said, not speaking to a soul.
Then you quickly exit the metro train
To take on your next role.

Part 4

LOVERS

Proverbs 30:18–19 (NIV)

There are three things that are too amazing for me, four that I do not understand: the way of an eagle in the sky, the way of a snake on a rock, the way of a ship on the high seas, and the way of a man with a young woman.

Steal Away

By a Friend

Let's find the time to steal away,
Head to the mountains for half a day,

And be with each other for just a short while.
Let me hold you and make you smile.

Have a lot of romance and wine.
Just being with you makes time divine.

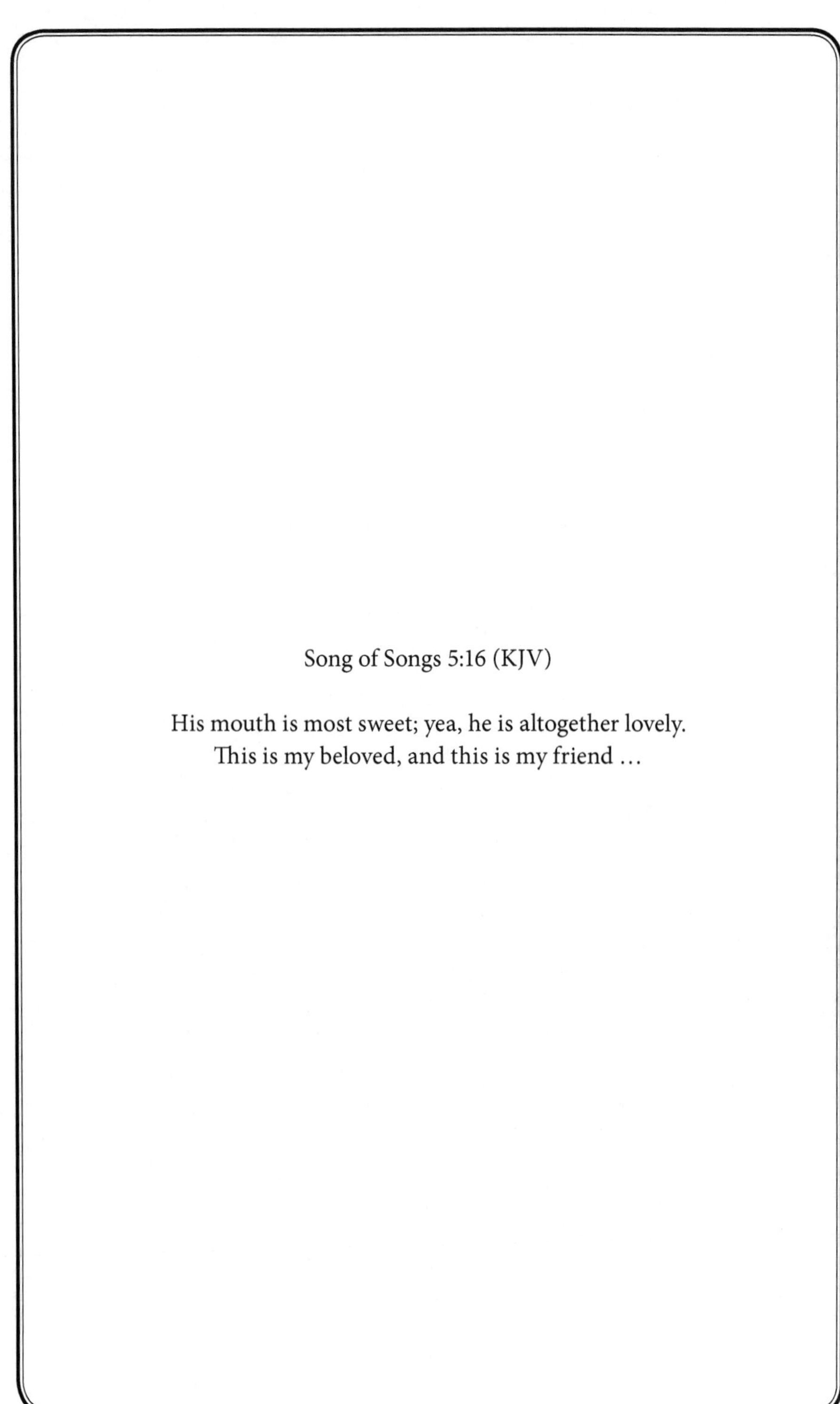

Song of Songs 5:16 (KJV)

His mouth is most sweet; yea, he is altogether lovely.
This is my beloved, and this is my friend …

He

By a Friend

He came quietly like a soft breeze, like a warm whisper.

He slipped inside my head and began to turn the pages.

He pressed his heart against my heart, his smile against my smile.

He sat down in the middle of my soul, and Christmas came early.

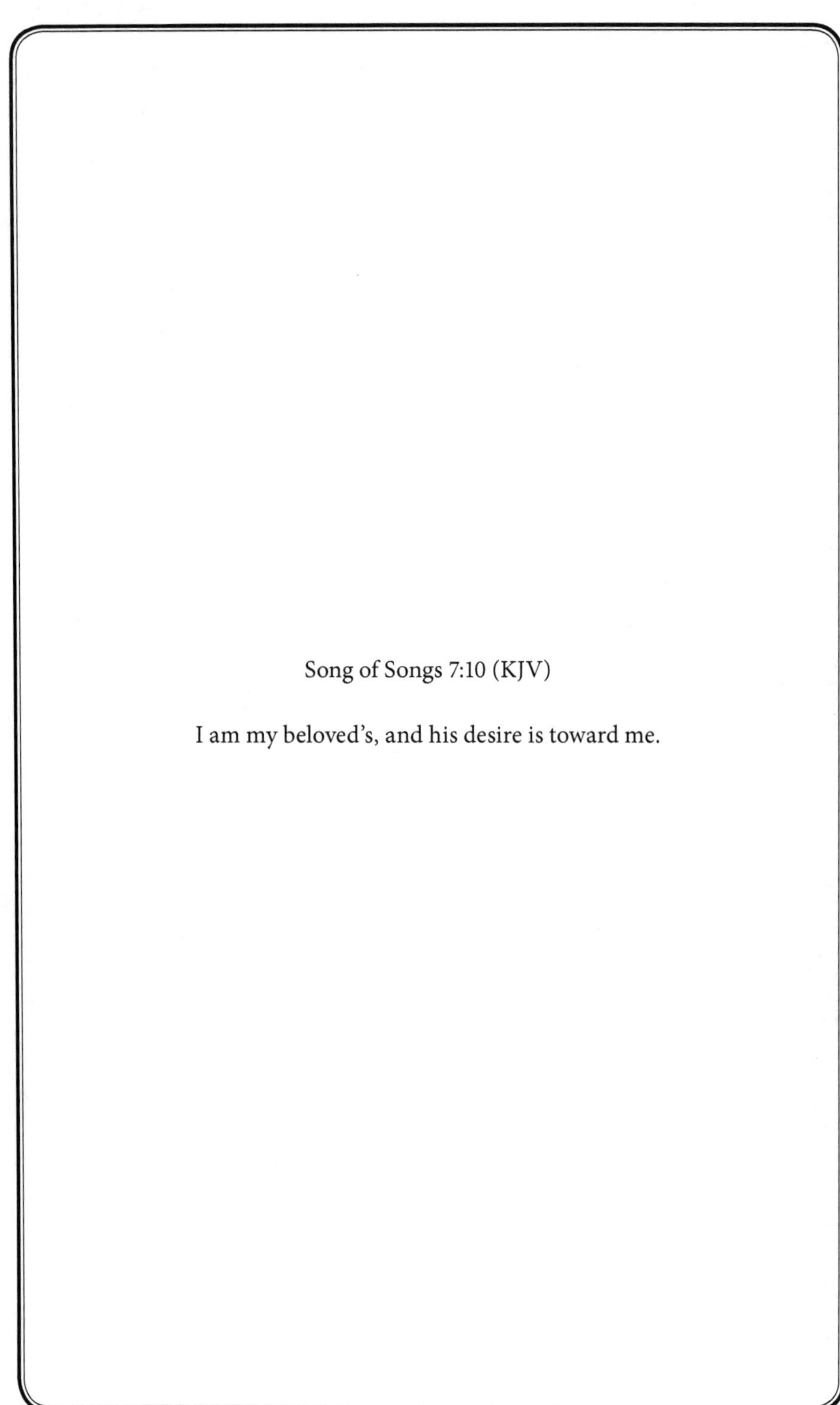

Song of Songs 7:10 (KJV)

I am my beloved's, and his desire is toward me.

Not Enough Time

By a Friend

Not enough time to fool around.
Not enough time to get on down.

Not enough time except to pass and stare.
Not enough time to show how much we care.

Not enough time to kick back and be hazy.
Not enough time to let loose and get crazy.

Part 5

THE TWO BECOME ONE

Song of Songs 4:9–10 (ESV)

You have captivated my heart, my sister, my bride; you have captivated my heart with one glance of your eyes, with one jewel of your necklace. How beautiful is your love, my sister, my bride! How much better is your love than wine, and the fragrance of your oils than any spice!

Falling and Staying in Love

No one falls in love by choice;
It is by chance.

No one stays in love by chance;
It is by work.

And no one falls out of love by chance;
It is by choice.

Proverbs 5:18–19 (NIV)

May your fountain be blessed, and may you rejoice in the wife of your youth. A loving doe, a graceful deer—may her breasts satisfy you always, may you ever be intoxicated with her love.

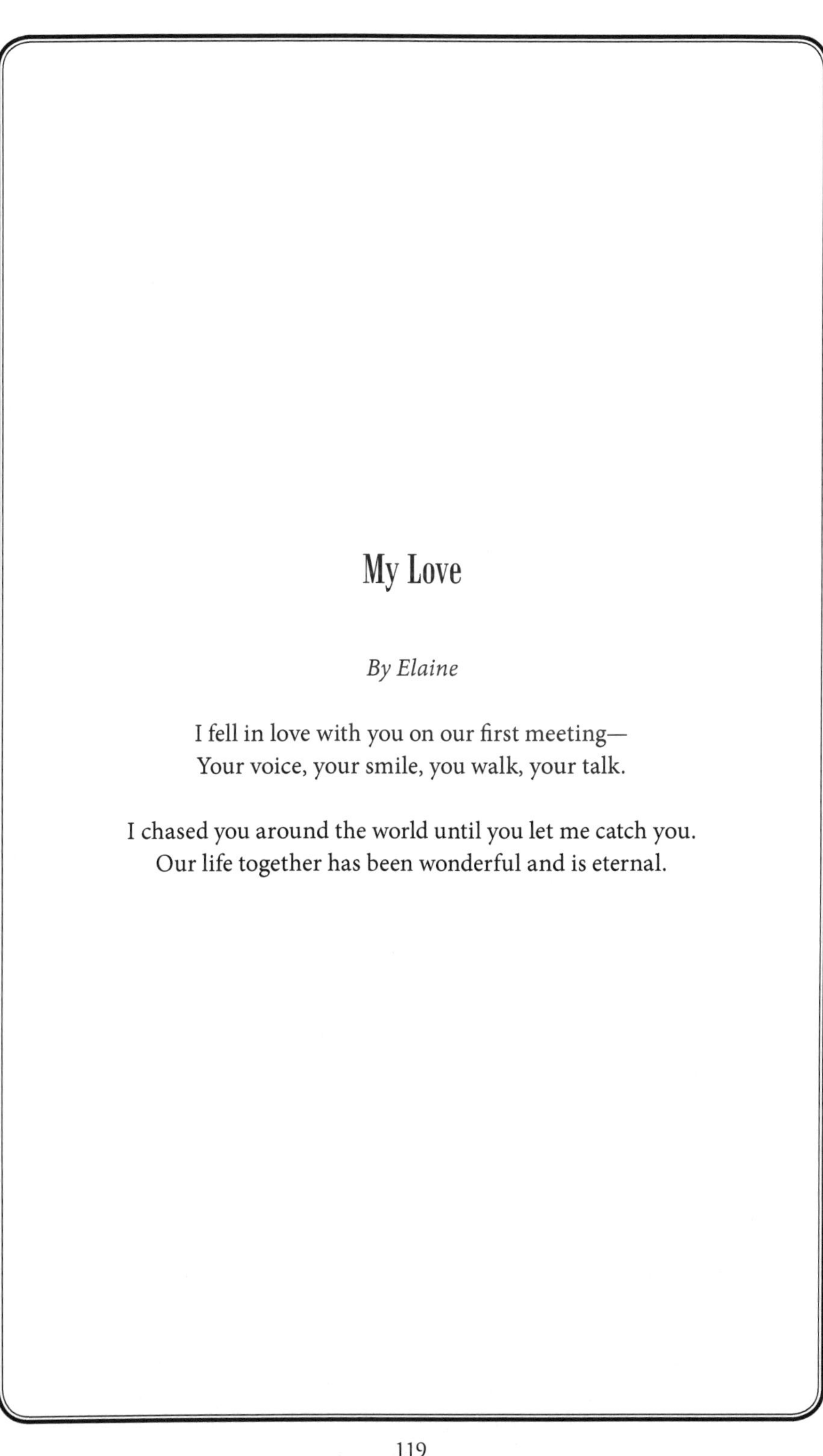

My Love

By Elaine

I fell in love with you on our first meeting—
Your voice, your smile, you walk, your talk.

I chased you around the world until you let me catch you.
Our life together has been wonderful and is eternal.

Proverbs 3:15 (NIV)

She is more precious than rubies; nothing you desire can compare with her.

WIFE

My very best friend, you know me so well.
You keep God first, and everyone can tell.

Your caring, sharing, counseling too
Motivate me; that's really what you do.

You always amaze me; I give you much respect.
I'm totally in love with my Woman in Full Effect!

Proverbs 18:22 (ESV)

He who finds a wife finds a good thing and obtains favor from the Lord.

Married

I'm a married man,
And I'm happy too.
She's more than enough;
No, I don't need two.

I put my trust in God.
Yes, I believe in Him.
Asked Him for a woman, a lover, and a friend.
And He sent her to me
Like He said He would.
And I promised on my knees
To always treat her good.

No, I don't need Liz, and I don't need Pam.
I'm more than happy just the way that I am.
True, I sometimes look, but I would never touch,
'Cause I will never violate her trust.

So I thank You, God,
For showing how much You care
By sending one of Your angels
Down here for me to share.

Proverbs 31:11–12 (KJV)

The heart of her husband doth safely trust in her, so that he shall have no need of spoil. She will do him good and not evil all the days of her life.

Don't Give Up on Me

I am not the best me
I know I can be,
So trust in me a little longer
With a strong attitude.
I refuse to lose;
I've got this burning hunger.

I won't betray your trust.
Believe me, I'm no wanderlust.
I'm focused on my goal.
I'm a champion in my soul;
My heart is right.
I have success in sight.

I appreciate all your support.
You always praise me and lift me up.
It's so good to see
You're right here for me.
I remember where I came from.
Know that the best is yet to come.

From time to time, I get down,
But I am never, ever through.
No time for a pity party—
There's still much work to do.

I celebrate little victories
And learn from every stumble.
Try never to become so arrogant
That I forget to be humble.

I'm in this race through His divine grace.
Please, don't give up on me.

Proverbs 31:10 (KJV)

Who can find a virtuous woman? For her price is far above rubies.

Yet to Come

Nine to five is not enough;
I know I must labor longer.
So many things left to obtain,
And I must feed this hunger.

I hope that you can feel and see
Where I am coming from,
And know I do this all for you.
The best is yet to come.

Part 6

AN IMPERISHABLE INHERITANCE

John 3:16 (KJV)

For God so loved the world, that he gave his only begotten Son, that whosoever believeth in him should not perish, but have everlasting life.

James 4:14 (KJV)

Whereas ye know not what shall be on the morrow. For what is your life? It is even a vapour, that appeareth for a little time, and then vanisheth away.

Old

I just happened to meet Mr. Old one morning,
standing there in my bathroom mirror.
As I stared into that strange looking face, I had so much to consider.

How on earth did you get here so quickly? There is still so much to be done.
I was so sure I had a plethora of days remaining here under the sun.

But there he stood, just staring at me, with wonder on his face,
Asking how could I be so surprised that I was nearing the end of the race.

"It's much too soon, too much to do. You know I need more time!"
But he just sadly shook his head, saying, "I can't give what is not mine."

So there I stood, staring at this mirror, wondering what to do.
Gather ye rosebuds while ye may; this world is not long … for you.

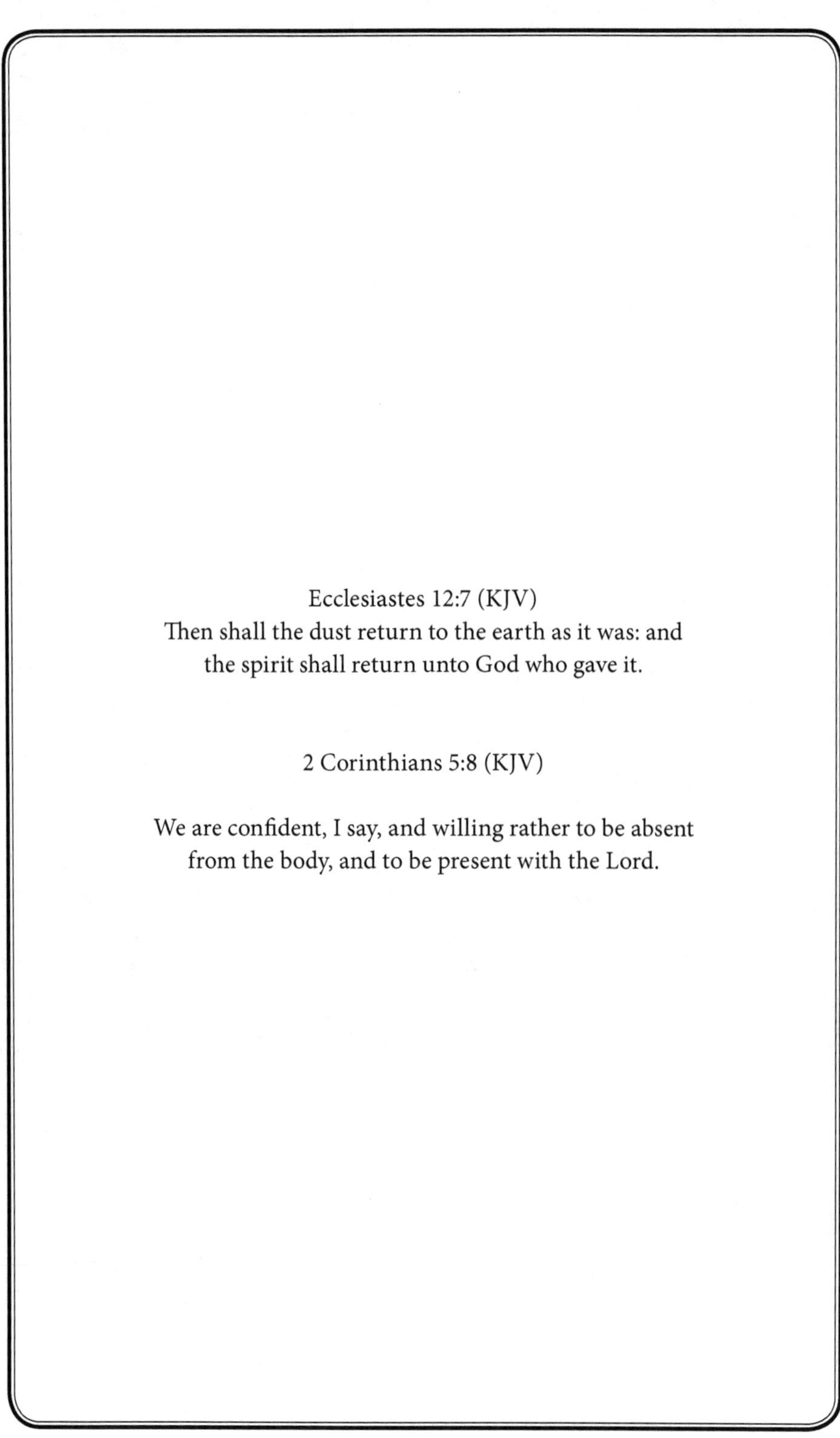

Ecclesiastes 12:7 (KJV)
Then shall the dust return to the earth as it was: and the spirit shall return unto God who gave it.

2 Corinthians 5:8 (KJV)

We are confident, I say, and willing rather to be absent from the body, and to be present with the Lord.

Empty

Imagine living your life on full,
Each day an adventure to look forward to.
Enjoying every day spent on this earth
Taking only joy with us when we return to dirt.

Making sure the people you know
Knows their special place in your heart and soul,
Traveling to places in far-off lands,
Drinking in God's wonders, holding a lover by the hand.

Special times shared with family and friends;
Days filled with joy from beginning to end.
Until the day when the end does come;
When your tank is empty, your race has been run.

And you think, *Lord, I've seen all I can see.*
My tank is empty now. May I walk with Thee?

Revelation 14:13 (ESV)

And I heard a voice from heaven saying, "Write this: Blessed are the dead who die in the Lord from now on." "Blessed indeed," says the Spirit, "that they may rest from their labors, for their deeds follow them!

Alarm Clocks

God sets two alarm clocks
Inside each one of us:
The first when we come into this world;
The last when we return to dust.

It's as if on the first bell,
He sends us out to play
Until His second bell calls us home
To His kingdom, where we will stay.

Everyone's time is different;
Some much longer than others.
Sometimes He calls the children first;
Sometimes He calls the mothers.

No one can ever really know
The ways of His master plan.
The only thing we know for sure
Is one day we all leave this land.

So run out on that first bell
And live life joyful and full.
Don't worry about the second bell;
You may never hear His pull.

Just know one day the Father
Is going to call you home.
There's no need to fear or worry.
You will never walk alone.

John 14:1–3 (NIV)

Let not your heart be troubled; you believe in God, believe also in Me. In My Father's house are many mansions; if it were not so, I would have told you. I go to prepare a place for you. And if I go and prepare a place for you, I will come again and receive you to Myself; that where I am, there you may be also.

Don't Worry

Don't worry about the failures you have in your life,
For we are all failures in our walk into the light.
When each of our final roll call has come,
There will be many things still left undone.

No matter how much you do and see,
You can't possibly see or do it all.
You won't realize how much was missed
Until your final curtain call.

Concentrate on the things that you can do,
And all the lives you touch while you're here.
Try to keep all relationships positive,
Especially with those you hold dear.

John 10:27–29 (KJV)

My sheep hear my voice, and I know them, and they follow me. I give them eternal life, and they will never perish, and no one will snatch them out of my hand. My Father, who has given them to me, is greater than all, and no one is able to snatch them out of the Father's hand. (Jesus speaking)

Home-Going

I once went to a funeral,
Where a home-going celebration broke out.
Instead of folks wailing and crying,
They began to sing and shout.

The preacher began to expound
On the glory of being called home,
For not everyone is going to be called
On the rolls of the kingdom throne.

Mourning comes with an expiration date
'Cause troubles don't last always.
Happiness has an activation date,
And joy comes with the morning sun's rays.

The family, though feeling the loss,
Was also filled with a special joy.
And with every song the choir sang,
Their spirits were lifted even more.

Friends just turned out in droves
To give their final testimony
Of everlasting relationships
And how important friendship can be.

The ride to the gravesite bought reflections
Of meetings, especially the first,
And a momentary lapse of sadness
Viewing the taillights of the hearse.

As we gathered around the coffin,
The heavens appeared to part,
And a voice from above touched us all
Tenderly, right in the heart.

"Worry not, friends and family, as this body is returned to dirt.
For lo, I'm with him always, even to the ends of the earth."
So celebrate, don't cry, when the angel of mercy comes.
For the departed are now on streets of gold; our time is yet to come!

Part 7

MORE OF BURTON'S WISDOM

Proverbs 27:17 (NIV)

As iron sharpens iron, so one person sharpens another.

Burton's Wisdom on Friends and More

Proverbs says, "A mirror reflects a man's face, but what he is really like is shown by the kind of friends he chooses." The simple but true fact of life is that you become like those with whom you closely associate—for the good and the bad.

If you were to list your greatest benefits, resources, or strengths, you would find that money is one of the least important ones, and some of your greatest resources are the people you know. A true friend sees beyond you to what you can be.

Most people live in minutes. I choose to live in moments. My military life changed the moment I met Jim Oden. My personal life changed again the moment I met Elaine.

As you grow, your associates will change. Some of your friends will not want you to go on. They will want you to stay where they are. Friends who don't help you climb will want you to crawl. Your friends will stretch your vision or choke your dream. Bottom line: those who don't increase you will eventually decrease you.

Consider this: never receive counsel from unproductive people. Never discuss your problems with someone incapable of contributing to the solution, because those who never succeed themselves are always first to tell you how. Not everyone has a right to speak into your life. You are certain to get the worst of the bargain when you exchange ideas with the wrong person.

Don't follow anyone who's not going anywhere. With some people, you spend an evening; with others, you invest it. Be careful where you stop to inquire for directions along the road of life. Wise is the person who fortifies his life with the right friendships and continually invests in an evening!

Similarly, lighting another individual's candle doesn't dim your candle.

Lastly, it is important to remember that a mirror has two purposes: not only to reflect what's there but also for you to correct what's there!

Part 8

A SHORT STORY

Gabrielle

Gabrielle. Almost six hours of tracking, waiting, and hoping in this stifling heat, and finally she appears. She's not alone. There are a bevy of beauties with her, but even in this crowd, she stands out and demands all of my attention. I feel my heart race in anticipation. As I survey the scene, my pride is almost beyond containment. It is my pride that has bought me to this place on this particular day. There is a hunger within me that has gone unsatisfied for far too long. But no longer.

To the east, the sun is at meridian and is hot. Just north of my position, the soft, rolling sound of the water that has made its way from the huge river provides a cool resting place for groups to gather. Every since we were young, I have been enticed by Gabrielle, but I was never fortunate enough to have her for my prize. Of all my other conquests, none has overshadowed my overwhelming desire to have her. I have stalked her for what seems an eternity, but fate seems always to be against me. It was as if Gabrielle was taunting me without knowing it, and because she does not know that I have been stalking her all this time, the chase is both frustrating … and exciting. In truth, this is as close as I've ever come, and the feeling is intoxicating!

"Steady," I hear the command sound in my head as I will myself to be calm, be patient. This is not the time to become restless. My pride will not stand for a loss at this critical juncture. I stay low and out of sight, careful not to make the slightest sound. I use the natural cover of the tall grass for concealment.

"How long are we going to stay here, Gabrielle?" That's Crystal, Gabrielle's closest friend and constant companion.

"What's the rush? It's cool here. We'll leave in a few minutes," Gabrielle replies. There's no mistaking who the leader of this group is; she simply carries herself in such a manner to demand respect. Even my respect. She is a prize I shall long treasure.

I can sense from my pride that it is time to move. Then, without warning, Gabrielle's head comes up. Smoke. She can smell it on the warm, west wind, and she knows that hunters are near. I smell it too, and like Gabrielle, I know that the hunters are near, but not too close to interfere with these carefully laid plans.

"Remember to always be careful," Father told me. "You are the perfect predator, but stealth must ever be your watchword. If you are discovered, you may become the hunted." But not today. Today, Gabrielle and her friends are my prey. Today, the bloodlust is upon me. Today, I will not be denied!

Ever so slowly, I circle to the east to stay upwind of the beauties. My pride is calm and under control; everything is going strictly by the numbers. My mouth waters, and I know that the time to strike is now, while they are completely unaware and vulnerable. My nostrils flare, the hairs on the nape of my neck bristle, every sense is on red alert, and I am ready to pounce.

Upon raising my head, I feel the steamy breeze tingle my nostrils. The time has come. I turn to look over my left shoulder to ensure all areas are covered. It is time to strike … now!

I move slowly so as not to reveal my presence too soon. To my surprise, Gabrielle and her companions jump in unison and take off in a mad dash of desperation. Through the shallow part of the water, they are a blur, heading west with speed born of survival fear. I am in hot pursuit when I hear it. There is an ever-increasing whistle and the *whop-whop* of propeller blades. Human hunters using a helicopter!

Up ahead I see one of Gabrielle's friends go down in a heap even before I hear the high-powered rifle. With my pride, I stop and retreat to the concealing cover of the tall grass as more shots are sounded. The same grass that concealed me from Gabrielle now protects me from these new predators. Fate has denied me again!

I whisper a silent prayer that Gabrielle is all right, that she is not taken. For she is my prize; she belongs to me. Why? Because this is Africa, and I am the greatest hunter in Africa. For the rest of the lionesses in my pride and for myself, tomorrow is another day. Darwin had it right. Survival of the fittest is the law of the jungle, and I will survive. As for Gabrielle, tomorrow is another day.

Ecclesiastes 3:1–8 (NIV)
There is a time for everything, and a season for every activity under the heavens:

A time to be born and a time to die, a time to plant and a time to uproot;

A time to kill and a time to heal, a time to tear down and a time to build;

A time to weep and a time to laugh, a time to mourn and a time to dance;

A time to scatter stones and a time to gather them, a time to embrace and a time to refrain from embracing;

A time to search and a time to give up, a time to keep and a time to throw away;

A time to tear and a time to mend, a time to be silent and a time to speak;

A time to love and a time to hate, a time for war and a time for peace.

Ecclesiastes 12:13 (KJV)
Let us hear the conclusion of the whole matter: Fear God and keep his commandments: for this is the whole duty of man.

Closing Comments

This earthly life is nothing less than the sum total of our thoughts, influences, choices-and-consequences, and other life events. These experiences —physical, emotional, and spiritual are stored in our memory vaults, define who we are, and are often modeled by others. Therefore, I deeply encourage you to live each day to inspire!

"Be the change that you wish to see in the world."
—Mahatma Gandhi

Made in the USA
Middletown, DE
07 August 2017